1

Ghosts of Franklin

Tennessee's Most Haunted Town

Margie Gould Thessin

Cover design: Andy Mangrum
Editor: René Evans
Layout and design: Anne Thessin and Margie Thessin

Front cover: Carnton Plantation, Photograph © Amy Price
Back cover: Sallie Carter, photograph courtesy of Winder Heller
Photograph page 25 courtesy of Ewing M. Braunig
Photographs pages 16, 17, 30, 33, 38, 40, 45, 74, 78, 82, 83,
85, 91, 96, 102, 111, 117, 122, 123, 127, 142, 149, 152, 159,
160, 163, 166, 176, 177, 182 by the author
Photographs pages 23, 43, 54, 59, 87, 93, 100, 118, 119
courtesy of Rick Warwick, the Heritage Foundation of Franklin
and Williamson County
Photographs pages 70 and 72 courtesy of Kelly Harwood
Photographs pages 134 and 137 courtesy of Carnton Plantation
Photograph page 179 by Molly Thessin

ISBN 1434899829
EAN-13 9781434899828
Second Printing, May, 2008
Third Printing, October, 2008
Fourth printing, November, 2009
Fifth printing, December, 2009
Sixth printing, August, 2011
Seventh printing, September, 2012

CONTENTS

Ghosts of Franklin

Tennessee's Most Haunted Town

DEDICATION

To my wonderful and supportive husband Mark and children Anne, Tyler and Molly and son-in-law Ryan;

To René Evans, great friend and former best business partner ever;

Special thanks to Laura Baxter, Denny Blake, Jeri Cameron, June Cameron, Cathy Clarkson, Marianne DeMeyers, John, Liz and Josh Ely, David Garrett, Gary and Katherine Harmon, Kelly Harwood, Angie Johnson, Sandra Kiger, Tom Lawrence, Pam Lewis, Eddie Martin, Heather Martin, Jim McReynolds, Carter Page, Allie Pierce, Tom Pierce, Amy Price, Lauren Rauter, Fred and Linda Reynolds, Shelly Robertson, J.D. Ryan, Jim and Becky Short, Ron Shuff, Shelley Snow, Susan Andrews Thompson, J. T. Thompson, Rusty Womack and everybody who didn't want their name used but told me their story anyway; and Joel Tomlin, who lit a fire under me to complete this project.

INTRODUCTION

HAUNTED HOUSES

By Henry Wadsworth Longfellow
1858

All houses wherein men have lived and died
  Are haunted houses. Through the open doors
The harmless phantoms on their errands glide,
  With feet that make no sound upon the floors.

We meet them at the doorway, on the stair,
  Along the passages they come and go,
Impalpable impressions on the air,
  A sense of something moving to and fro.

There are more guests at table, than the hosts
  Invited; the illuminated hall
Is thronged with quiet, inoffensive guests
  As silent on the pictures on the wall

The stranger at my fireside cannot see
  The forms I see, nor hear the sounds I hear;
He but perceives what is, while unto me
  All that has been is visible and clear.

We have no title-deeds to house or lands;
  Owners and occupants of earlier dates
From graves forgotten stretch their dusty hands,
  And hold in mortmain still their old estates.

The spirit-world around this world of sense
  Floats like an atmosphere, and everywhere
Wafts through these earthly mists and vapors dense
  A vital breath of more ethereal air.

Our little lives are kept in equipoise
  By opposite attractions and desires;
The struggle of the instinct that enjoys,
  And the more noble instinct that aspires.

These perturbations, this perpetual jar
  Of earthly wants and aspirations high,
Come from the influence of an unseen star,
  An undiscovered planet in our sky.

And as the moon from some dark gate of cloud
  Throws o'er the sea a floating bridge of light,
Across whose trembling planks our fancies crowd
  Into the realm of mystery and night,--

So from the world of spirits there descends
  A bridge of light, connecting it with this,
O'er whose unsteady floor, that sways and bends,
  Wander our thoughts above the dark abyss.

Henry Wadsworth Longfellow, author of *Paul Revere's Ride*, *Evangeline*, *The Courtship of Miles Standish* and *Song of Hiawatha*, was 19th century America's most popular poet. He based his poems on historical events, myths and legends, and became an icon of popular culture. He reminded Americans of their roots. He wrote for the masses and about the topics that interested ordinary people. Certainly *Haunted Houses* is not Longfellow's best-known work. Nevertheless it was apparently a topic of interest and so he wrote about it.

Until the modern age many people in diverse cultures believed in ghosts and spirits. Belief in otherworldly phenomena was not considered a sign of ignorance, stupidity or superstition. Ancient texts, including the Bible, include references to ghosts. After Jesus's resurrection, when He appeared to his disciples they thought they were "seeing a ghost." Jesus asked them, "Look at my hands and feet, that it is I myself. Touch me and see, because a ghost does not have flesh and bones as you can see I have." (Lk. 24:39) Shakespeare created the most famous ghost in literature, Hamlet's father. Hamlet tells the skeptic Horatio, "There are more things in heaven and earth, Horatio, than are dreamt of in your philosophy."

It's only in our modern, scientific world that even considering the possibility of the supernatural tags one as suggestible and simple-minded in some quarters. Science reigns supreme today. In the words of one former skeptic, "If science wasn't proving it, I wasn't buying it."

I was one of those skeptics. I'd never seen a ghost or anything approximating one. No mainstream scientist ever offered empirical, objective proof, accepted by the scientific community. Therefore, in my mind, it couldn't be true.

It wasn't until I founded (with friend and former business partner René Evans) Franklin on Foot that I even had an interest in the subject.

Franklin on Foot came about because René and I both volunteered with the Heritage Foundation of Franklin and Williamson County's Heritage Classroom program, starting back in the mid-'90s. The program provides programs on local history, including a downtown walking tour, to thousands of students every year.

When René and I realized there was interest among local folks as well as out-of-town visitors for the tour, we decided to start our little walking tour company, Franklin on Foot. It was only after certain people (you know who you are, Mary Pearce) suggested to us that we include a ghost tour that we even considered it.

"Ghost tour? But we don't know any ghost stories!" we told Mary, the Heritage Foundation's long-time executive director.

"Oh, just go talk to this person and that person," she told us. So off we went, making phone calls and knocking on doors of sane, ordinary folks who, it turns out, have either lived or worked or even just visited a building where they experienced strange and unaccountable events and phenomena that they can't explain by rational means. Before long, we had a huge collection of ghost stories told to us by very credible sources.

Our sources are not ghost hunters— measuring ectoplasm, taking temperature readings, and listening to EVPs—and neither are we!

I often get asked about my own personal experiences since I've started doing ghost tours. I also worked at Carnton

Plantation (See chapter 10) for almost five years, and developed a ghost tour there. I spent many a dark night in the house.

Sorry to disappoint, I have little to report. I think you have to be sensitive to it, and I guess I'm just insensitive. For my minor brush with the supernatural, see chapter 11.

That usually leads right back to, "Well, do you believe in ghosts?" Let's put it this way: I don't know exactly how to define these mysterious phenomena people describe in such exacting detail, but I do know what they're *not*. They're *not* the delusions of the insane or the products of over-active imaginations or the power of suggestion. Some enjoy "their" ghost but many are people who have had just one ghostly experience that they stumbled upon. They certainly don't relish it and often hope it will never happen again. One thing they all say in common, though is, "You can call me crazy but I know what I saw!"

I am not arrogant enough to think I know everything! I like to think there is some mystery left in life, and that's what these stories mean to me.

I hope you enjoy them as much as I do.

September, 2012

Chapter 1

The Original Steel Magnolia

It was approaching midnight on a swelteringly hot night in the summer of 1980. Shelley Snow, nationally-award-winning Tennessee oil and watercolor artist, was painting late in her studio at Shuff's Music Store, 118 Third Avenue North, Franklin. She was alone.

Shuff's Music had opened in 1978 in the elegant 19th century Greek Revival house in downtown. Ron Shuff, the owner and an accomplished musician himself, rents out the rooms in the house to music teachers, composers and musicians of all kinds, and also sells musical instruments, sheet music and supplies.

However, in the early days the studio was not fully rented with musicians, and when Shelley asked Ron to rent a room for her painting studio, he agreed.

Shelley was working late that night because she had a commissioned work on a deadline. As she worked later and later, she began to get sleepy. But with the deadline looming, she stayed at it. Finally, her eyelids heavy, she decided to take a nap on a couch she kept in the studio just for that purpose. She curled up and drifted off.

Suddenly, in the fog of sleep, Shelley heard a loud and unexpected sound. It went like this: crreeaak-crreeaak, crreeaak-crreeaak. Shelley sat up. Crreeaak-crreeaak, it continued. It wasn't coming from anywhere in the room.

Shelley, by now fully awake and listening intently, finally recognized the sound: it was the sound of a creaky old rocking chair. And somebody or something was rocking in it. But there was no rocking chair in Shuff's Music and no other person working that night either. Shelley had locked herself in the building and didn't see how there could be an intruder. The sound simply didn't make sense.

Nothing strange happens to most of the people who visit this building. But there are those few...

Shelley's first instinct was to bolt, but being naturally curious and unafraid, she followed the sound, passing through several rooms, and finally came upon its source. The creaking sound was coming from a room on the second floor overlooking the street. The door to the room was closed. Shelley eased open the door and peered into the room. There, in a room facing the street, gently rocking back and forth in a rocking chair by the window, was the spirit of a very old woman.

"She looked very wrinkly and tired," Shelley remembers, "and was wearing a long white gown and night cap."

The ancient specter continued her rocking: crreeaak - crreeaak, as she looked at Shelley, who was frozen to the spot and staring disbelievingly. Finally, the spirit spoke, and said, "I used to live in this house."

The spirit sat in a chair behind this door.

"I didn't know what to think!" Shelley said. "I kind of wanted to talk to her. But, instead I quickly closed the door, got my purse, and left."

Later, people suggested to Shelley that it had all been a dream. She scoffs at that theory, saying, "The memory is as clear to me now as it was when it happened in 1980. How many dreams can you say that about?"

"The only thing I regret is that I didn't stay and talk to her," Shelley said recently. I told her, "Shelly, we all regret that you didn't stay and talk to her! We would love to have heard what else she had to say!"

Who was this apparition claiming erstwhile residence of the house on Third Avenue? Evidence points to one of the original steel magnolias, a woman named Sallie Ewing Sims Carter Gaut.

Sallie, born Sarah Ann, was born in 1826 into one of Franklin's founding families, the Ewings of Murfreesboro Road.

High birth and wealth did not protect her from tragedy; she was orphaned at 12 years of age. Described once as "quite a belle with the young boys," Sallie married at the age of 15 and had three children. She was widowed for the first time at just 23. Engaged to be married again, the fascinating young widow attended a soiree where she met dashing Winchester, Tennessee lawyer Joseph Carter, also engaged to be married. They fell madly in love, broke off their respective engagements, and married. Sadly, after two more children and just four years of marriage, Sallie once again wore widow's weeds.

Sallie was living in the house at 118 Third Avenue North with her four surviving children when the Civil War broke out. A self-proclaimed "intense secessionist," Sally was heartbroken when the Union army, after capturing Nashville, marched 15 miles south to occupy Franklin.

The beautiful and daring Sallie Carter led an interesting life. Colonel Baxter Smith (C.S.A.) described her as "young, handsome, sprightly and possessed of extraordinary tact." Sallie's own memoir was entitled: "The Times That Tried Men's Souls—and Women's As Well."

Life changed overnight. The army commandeered the county courthouse on the town square for use as its headquarters, and built a fort on a hill overlooking town. Fort Granger, named for its commanding general Gordon Granger, held a garrison of as many as 8,000 soldiers. Sentries were posted at all the roads in and out of town. To leave town civilians were required to seek permission and a pass from General Granger, who had the power to ask one's destination and business. How infuriating! But what could Sallie Carter do about it?

After all, she was female and a woman couldn't be a soldier. She was a widow with four children and had her hands full. She was 38, which in those days meant practically dead.

Oh, Sallie figured something out. She became a spy.

Spying was (and is) serious business. Convicted of espionage, a spy could expect to be swinging from the end of a rope by daybreak the next morning.

But when life as you know it is threatened, you take chances. So Sallie began gathering information in various ways, from the simple act of counting soldiers marching through town to inviting Union officers to her house for dinner. She was, in the words of a Union soldier, "one of the famous beauties in Middle Tennessee." Nobody would turn down that invitation. And after a little liquor was poured into the evening, sometimes information was inadvertently leaked.

But now for the hard part: passing the information out of town. There was that pesky matter of a pass and the nosy sentry. But Sallie was not deterred. She simply hid notes in her clothing, her hair and even in the hollowed-out cork of a whiskey bottle, which she then offered as a bribe to the sentry. And off she went.

Once on a trip to Nashville, Sallie was arrested, taken to the Federal headquarters and questioned about Confederate activities around Franklin. She said nothing, but played her ace in the hole. Turns out Sallie wasn't just beautiful, charming and brainy, she was also connected, in this case by blood to a Union army officer, former Tennessee governor William Campbell, who vouched for her and secured her release. When she asked Cousin Will for a pass home, he refused, and explained that the Union army was planning an attack on Murfreesboro that night and it would be dangerous for Sallie—she might get caught in the middle of the conflict.

Now Sallie *had* to get home and tell what she had just learned from her unwitting Cousin Will. So she hired a man with a horse and buggy and sneaked out of Nashville, going through gates and woodlands, evading scouts and pickets, finally arriving at a place where she could pass the information. All in a day's work.

The Battle of Franklin was terrifying for the citizens of Franklin. And afterwards, Sallie's house was used as a hospital for both Union and Confederate soldiers.

Sallie, now Mrs. Gaut, in late middle age

After four long years of strife and conflict, terror and bloodshed, the war ended. Sallie was unhappy with the outcome, but just glad it was over.

Later Sallie married Judge John C. Gaut, moved to Nashville with him, and was widowed for the third and final time after 18 years of marriage. She returned to her Franklin house where she lived out her years with her daughter, one of two surviving children. In 1912, now a very old woman, Sallie died at the age of 87.

Was Sallie the spirit that so startled Shelley Snow so many years ago? Ron Shuff thinks so.

One day shortly after he started the business, Ron was visited by a "wild-eyed" stranger. A self-proclaimed clairvoyant, she proclaimed that the house had "great charisma" because of a spirit who was present there. She added that she—the spirit— would be helpful if Ron let her.

Ron didn't know about that, because pictures and a large mirror had a very unhelpful way of dropping off the walls and flying across the room. But Sallie Carter could certainly claim great charisma and had a long history and attachment to the house.

As time passed, more and more strange and unexplainable stories emerged.

A musician popped his head out the door at Shuff's one fall evening several years ago.

"What are you all doing out here?" he asked me. He wasn't unfriendly, just curious why people were paying such rapt attention to the lady in the hoop skirt.

"Just doing a ghost tour," I told him.

"I wonder if Ron ever told you about my ghost," he said.

"Don't think so. Do tell," I encouraged him.

Ray, we'll call him, had been a tenant at Shuff's for about six months the first time *it* happened. He was working late one night, composing at the piano in his studio, when a young woman passed behind him. She was dressed, he said, pointing at me in my hoop skirt, "like you," and floated rather than walked.

"I got up from my piano and followed her into the room she'd gone into, but she'd disappeared," Ray said. "I said to myself, 'I've really got to go home and get some sleep. I'm hallucinating.'"

And he put it out of his mind . . . until it happened again about a year later.

This time Ray said to himself, "I'm really seeing her. This is not my mind playing tricks. I'm seeing a ghost."

She visited Ray about eight times over ten years. There were times when Ray couldn't actually see her, but he said he knew it was the same spirit.

Hmm . . . I asked Ray, "If you couldn't see her, how do you know it was a 'her'?"

"I could smell her perfume," he asserted. "And it wasn't a modern scent like women today wear, it was old-fashioned and flowery like your grandmother's."

Ray isn't afraid of this young woman who floats in and out of his studio in the middle of the night. Ray says, "I'm a musician. I work late. It's usually 2:00-3:00 a.m. when she appears and I always take that as a sign to go home to my wife."

Soldiers Still Stand at Attention

Sallie Carter entertained and cared for both Union and Confederate soldiers in the house and it appears that both armies are still represented at Shuff's.

A teenager and her mother came to Shuff's to buy a trumpet in the mid-1990s. As they were walking up the front steps, the young woman saw the ghost of a Confederate soldier standing next to the front door. She looked at her mother as if to say, "Whoa!" but by the time she looked back, he had disappeared. By the time they entered the building he was standing in the corner, and then slowly dissipated.

A man on a tour told me he was driving down Third Avenue one night, idly looking around, and noticed the ghost of a Civil War soldier looking out the window. He wasn't so shocked to see a ghost, he said, but asked, "Why is there a ghost of a *Union* soldier in this town?" Obviously he didn't know his history, so I filled him in.

One brisk fall night in 2007 I was telling my group about the description several people have used when they've heard "footsteps." They'll say, "Ok, it's an old house, it's going to creak. But what I heard was so *deliberate*; it wasn't just the shifting and settling of an old house." At that, a musician who was standing outside Shuff's talking on his cell phone, interrupted me and said, "That's exactly right! That's the word I use to describe what happened to me here not long ago. Deliberate!"

Sallie Carter's house on Third Avenue bears little resemblance to the building's appearance today. Sallie, pictured sitting here with her daughter and granddaughter, still has a commanding appearance. "Mrs. Richardson," written on the photo, is her daughter.

Jeff, we'll call him, was the last person in the building one night and was circulating through the house to turn off lights. He was in an upstairs hall, and came upon a room with the door closed. He mused aloud to himself, "I wonder if there's a light on in there." Immediately, the door opened; the light was on. He turned it off. The room was empty.

"The door opening was so clearly in response to my question that I know something is in this house making it happen," he said. "It was deliberate!"

So . . . is it brave, beautiful, tactful, helpful, loyal Sallie Carter? Sometimes it's hard to tell, especially when things happen that seem out of character.

Several Januarys ago, it was the job of a high school student hired as a gopher to take down and box Christmas decorations and haul them up to the attic. He carried one box up the pull-down attic stairs, and placed the box all the way across the room in the corner. He came down the stairs, picked up the other box on the first floor, and went back to the room to the pull-down stairs. There, dumped all over the floor, were the Christmas decorations. He said it was as if someone had kicked the box all the way across the attic floor and down the stairs.

A Sallie Carter descendant from Atlanta came on a tour several years ago and proclaimed, "It's Aunt Sis!" when she heard about some of the mischievous activity in the house. She said that Sallie's daughter-in-law Narcissa "Sis" Carter lived with Sallie after her husband, Sallie's son, died. According to this relative, she was not a nice person. In fact, when she died no one came forth to pay for a tombstone, and to this day, she's buried in an unmarked grave.

Ron thinks "activity" in the building has died down in recent years. However, during "ghost tour season" in October of 2009, I was conducting a tour and of course, visited Shuff's. It was a weeknight, and a parade of teachers and students passed in and out of the door.

A guitar teacher stopped and asked the group, "Do you want to hear my ghost story?" Well, you know the answer to that one. You betcha! She told us that while giving a ten-year-old boy a guitar lesson recently, a picture hanging between them on the wall, detached itself from its hanger and flew across the room.

The teacher said, "I looked at him; he looked at me, then he said, 'You don't see *that* every day.'" And then we continued our lesson."

Chapter 2

A Great Place to Live

Franklin, Tennessee, is a very nice town. I was about to say "small" town, but it's not small really, not anymore. There are about 68,000 people living here as of 2012 and another 100,000 in the surrounding county. Most of them came from other places which sometimes irritates the natives, but that's what happens when you have a great town. People want to live in it.

The reason they move here are the typical ones: jobs, schools, housing, the usual. Then there is the intangible that draws them here, what I call the "ahhhh" moment. It's that moment when they first come upon Franklin's town square and take in the view. They see the old Greek Revival-style courthouse with its cast iron columns and gingerbread-decorated Victorian stores and offices. Church steeples peek over the treetops and one lone neon drug store sign reminds viewers of an earlier time on Main Streets everywhere. In the center, in the middle of a greensward, the memorial statue of an unnamed Confederate soldier looks down on it all. It's that "small-town feeling" they get, which is why I started to describe

The Confederate monument and four Civil War-era cannons—
manufactured in Massachusetts—watch over Franklin's town square.

Franklin as small when it's really not. It's just that feeling. I see it on their faces all the time giving walking tours.

It's uncanny.

So, it's established, people like to live here.

Guess what? Some never want to leave . . . even after they die. Sometimes they get so attached to their houses that they hang around long after the funeral, years and years later, still making their presence known on occasion to startled occupants and visitors.

In 1999, Heather and Eddie Martin purchased a lovely 1880s house at 218 Third Avenue North from the estate of a much-loved local photographer who had used the house as his studio. The Martins' plan was to completely restore the house and use it as their offices—he was a financial planner and she ran an art gallery—and rent out another room as an office.

One morning Eddie arrived at the house, ready to begin work. He went to the front door, the only door they were using during the restoration, and discovered it was chained from the inside.

Well! This was odd. As usual, the house's other two doors were also chained from the inside. They weren't using those doors because there was a lot of stuff piled in front of them. So how did the front door get chained? Eddie and Heather had no explanation for it. It was impossible, and also weird.

Once they completed the restoration, the Martins moved into their offices. At the same time, they rented another room in the house to a graphic designer named Pete.

The Martins found an old Chamber of Commerce plaque in the basement. They learned that it had been awarded in the 1930s to a prominent Chamber of Commerce member who once owned the house, and who for some reason, didn't take it when he moved. One Christmas, Eddie and Heather were addressing Christmas cards when the plaque, which they displayed on a table, flew across the room, almost hitting Heather.

Next, a heavy brass fireplace screen in an unoccupied room took flight from a non-working, sealed fireplace. Heather, Eddie and Pete all heard the crash and rushed to see it crushed and lying against the opposite wall.

Their interest piqued, the Martins decided to investigate the history of the house. After examining the property records they learned the house had been the site of a single tragic event.

For about a year in 1937-38, the house was the residence of Max and Lena Beasley and their seven children, who moved in on October 1, 1937. Just three-and-a-half months later, on January 14, 1938, Max sat down on the sofa in the front parlor one day as supper was being called, put a gun to his head and pulled the trigger. Times were tough during the Great Depression in a typical Southern town, and Mr. Beasley was apparently despondent, believing he could not afford to keep the house. The former owners, who had financed the house for the Beasleys, allowed Mrs. Beasley and her children to live in the house until September when they moved out.

That convinced Eddie and Heather that Mr. Beasley was the ghost. Max had found a way to keep his house.

Mr. Beasley had a way of making his presence known to the Martins' visitors and clients in the house. He messed with one of the ceiling fans in the center hall.

"When a client came in who Beasley didn't like, the fan would freakin' go crazy, wobbling back and forth and making noise," Eddie recalls. "All I would have to say was, 'Mr. Beasley,' and it would stop."

"I wasn't a ghost believer," Eddie said. "You start out saying 'What's going on?' but now I believe there are definitely spirits in the house."

One toilet flushed on its own. An upstairs bedroom light turned on every morning at 9 a.m. One day Heather was alone in the house when she heard someone running down the upstairs hall and a door slam. Heather knew no one else was there but she ran upstairs to check anyway. Sure enough. No one was there.

"There was a lot of noise upstairs always. Especially when we changed anything. That always brought on a lot of activity," Eddie said.

One spirit in this house communicates through the ceiling fan and seems to have quite a temper.

In 2002, Eddie and Heather and their children moved into the house to live. That required Pete to move out.

One of the movers Pete hired refused to enter the house because he said there were ghosts in the house.

Ghosts *plural?* Pete knew about—and actually enjoyed—Mr. Beasley, but another one?

Yes, the mover said. He pointed to the front room on the right.

"This is where Mr. Beasley is, and this," he said pointing to the room at the left, "is where SHE is."

In fact, a woman had died in that room.

That gave Pete the creeps.

The old stone-walled basement was perfect for a wine cellar, and Eddie began to install one. One day while Eddie was home alone working on it the slide lock on the basement door closed, locking Eddie in. Eddie waited hours for Heather to come home and unlock the door.

The property is beautifully landscaped, a good deal of it put in when the photographer used the garden for photography sessions, and then added to by the Martins. At times, the Martins would entertain on the back patio with guests, and the guests would inquire as to who else was in the house.

"Oh, there's no one else," they'd say.

"But it looked like we saw someone through the windows."

"No, there's no one there . . . ."

Often startled but never afraid, Eddie found the supernatural activity "fascinating. Just always wondering what he was going to do next."

A group of descendants of Max and Lena Beasley who once came on a Franklin on Foot ghost tour roared when they heard about the flying objects.

"What's funny?" I asked.

They looked at each other knowingly, and one said, "It has to be a Beasley in that house. All Beasleys throw things when they lose their temper!" (Author's apologies to all Beasleys who don't throw things when they lose their temper!)

In addition to the various manifestations of Mr. Beasley, Heather and Eddie once saw a strange dog in the house. Heather spotted it first, called out to Eddie, but by the time they got up from their chairs and ran to the hall, it had disappeared.

"It looked like Freeway," Heather said, referring to the dog belonging to the photographer who once owned the building. He brought him to work every day and Heather recognized him from times she had been at the studio having her children's pictures taken.

And when Freeway died, the photographer buried him in the backyard.

In 2004, Heather and Eddie sold the property to a woman who uses it as an event venue.

One night on my Franklin on Foot ghost tour, a guest named John happened to bring his dog along. The pooch, named Lucy, was on a leash and appeared to me to be very well behaved. After the tour, John asked me if I had noticed his dog's odd behavior. I hadn't; it was a very large group and I was too busy leading the tour to notice anything unusual.

Here's what happened: The group sat as usual on what was then an 18-inch high curb across the street from the house. Immediately Lucy began to growl. A few minutes into my story, the current owner came out of her house through the front door, waved at the group, got in her car and drove off. Lucy began to whimper and whine. She then jumped in John's lap, and stayed there until we moved to our next stop.

I told John that it seemed to me that Lucy was "seeing" something that the rest of us weren't. First, Lucy "saw" another dog through the glass front door on the house, which caused her to growl. When the woman opened the door, this phantom dog came outside and ran across the street to check out the interloper, which made Lucy whine and retreat to her owner's lap.

John said that's what it seemed like to him, too. That's exactly what dogs do!

Chapter 3

What's With Third Avenue, Anyway?

Third Avenue in downtown Franklin is part of the original 15-block town laid out in 1799 by Abram Maury.

Mr. Maury came to Franklin to establish a town on a land grant from the State of North Carolina. He had not actually been awarded the grant. Major Anthony Sharpe had received 8,760 acres of prime Tennessee land for Revolutionary War heroism. He sold Maury 640 acres of which 109 constitute the original town of Franklin.

Originally named Marthaville in honor of his wife Martha, Maury honored Benjamin Franklin instead when his reticent wife demurred. (The Marthaville story always gets a chuckle on walking tours. While women's names often serve for cities—think Charlotte, N.C. and Elizabeth, N.J.—Marthaville just doesn't quite have the right ring to it.)

Maury named the streets too. Following logic, he called the main east/west road Main Street and the main cross street Main Cross Street. Streets on the outside boundary, or margin of town, were called N., S., E. or W. Margin Streets.

Several churches were on Church Street, and the bridge was at the end of Bridge Street—but not anymore. Now it's on Main Street.

College Street had a school and Indigo Street a dye factory and Cameron Street got its name from the builder of the first house in town, Ewen Cameron. You get the picture.

Over the years, some street names have changed. Main

Cross became Maple and then Third. In fact all the east/west streets' names have changed over the years, going to an easier numbering system—when you've got *five whole blocks* in your town in either direction, you've got to keep it simple.

Coming from the south, Third Avenue crosses Main Street at the Public Square and continues two blocks where it runs right into the corner of the oldest public cemetery in town, appropriately named City Cemetery.

Is this why Third Avenue seems to have the highest concentration of haunted buildings of any street in the old downtown? Whatever the reason, it's one spirited street.

A Room with a View

Mrs. Nelle Mosley was the last person to live in the beautiful 1820s house located at 117 Third Avenue North. A widow, Mrs. Mosley shared the house with her sister until her sister passed away, then lived there alone after that. After she died in 1987 the house was put up for auction and Ron Shuff, across the street, bought the house and used it for a time as his piano showroom and for music lessons.

One day shortly after Ron had started using the building, one of his teachers, a music student at Belmont University, emerged from the Mosley house "like he'd been shot out of a cannon," said Ron, who happened to be standing on the porch of his main building at the time.

He asked the young man what the matter was, and the teacher said, firmly, "Ron, I'm not going to give my lessons over there anymore. I've got to give all my lessons over here. I just saw Mrs. Mosley!"

One night in late spring 2005, a woman ran out of the building and flagged down our ghost tour group as we were walking down Third Avenue in front of her store.

"Hey! Are you all doing that ghost tour?" she asked the group.

"Why, yes, we are!" one of the tour-goers answered for the group.

Mrs. Mosley hadn't been gone long when she appeared
to a young music teacher.

"Well I just saw my ghost! Want to come inside and hear about it?"

She didn't have to ask twice. Everybody was quite excited to be hearing a first-hand account of a sighting.

Joan, we'll call her, led us into the front room on the right. At the time, the building was empty. Joan was in the process of refurbishing it to open a home décor and gift shop called Franklin Marketplace. Here's what she told us:

"I walked into the room. It seemed that the air-conditioning had come on and it was freezing but I hadn't turned it on. I saw a figure in the room. She was sitting in a rocking chair in the corner of the room by the front windows. It was a misty figure, an apparition. I knew without a doubt it was a woman but I don't know why. And then I smelled cigar smoke."

Our group was quite impressed with the story, but unfortunately, the apparition had disappeared by the time we got there. Nevertheless, everyone said they got more than their money's worth that night.

Later Joan learned that Mrs. Mosley used the room, a front parlor, as her bedroom. She used to sit in a chair where she had a view out a window facing onto Third Avenue as well as a side window. She liked to watch the daily goings-on on Third Avenue and the town square. Reportedly, she occasionally enjoyed smoking a cigar.

After hearing that, the owner was convinced that Mrs. Mosley was the spirit inhabiting 117 Third Avenue North.

The following Christmas a woman we'll call Mary visited the store with her husband and two grown daughters. The next day, Mary and her husband returned without the daughters to purchase items the girls had picked out.

Mary asked Joan, who was manning the counter that day: "Do you know you have a ghost in this house?"

"Yes, I do! I think it's the former owner of the house, Mrs. Mosley. But how do you know that?" Joan answered.

"I just had a conversation with her," Mary explained. "I'm clairvoyant. I'm in contact with the 'other side' I am 'off duty' right now, but if you want me to help her move to the other side, I'll be happy to."

"I don't want you to do that. This is her house, too," the shop owner said. "But can you just tell me what is keeping Mrs. Mosley here?" she asked.

Mary answered, "She's living in limbo. Usually it's something they're hanging on to, maybe a loved one."

At that, she finished her shopping and left, leaving Mrs. Mosley a welcome presence to the present occupant.

A few minutes later, Mary came back and poked her head in the door. She told Joan: "I don't know what it is about this street . . . but there are at least a dozen spirits out here and they are all screaming at me to talk to them . . . but I'm off duty so I won't!"

Hmmm . . . just as we thought. Third Avenue's just a' crawling with ghosts!

The north side of Third Avenue seems to have a large concentration of ghosts, but not to slight the south side . . .

And Let There Be . . . Dark?

The red brick house at 224 Third Avenue South is Franklin's oldest downtown house, built circa 1805 by a Mr. Saunders. The federal-style dwelling is reminiscent of houses in Eastern seaboard cities such as Philadelphia, Boston and the Georgetown section of Washington, D.C.

Old-fashioned Park Marshall still doesn't care for the electricity in his old homeplace. And he's not shy about making his feelings known.

The house is now known as the Marshall House, after the well-known and respected Franklin lawyer and jurist John Marshall purchased it in 1844.

John's son Park was just a boy of nine when his father died in 1863. The very next year, the terrified family huddled in the cellar as the Battle of Franklin raged above them. It was an experience Park never forgot. He studied and wrote about the war for the rest of his life. A tangible reminder of the Battle of Franklin was the cannonball that struck the house, broke through the brick wall and splintered the back of a family armoire; for many years the heavy lead piece was used as a doorstop.

Park, a lawyer like his father, spent some of his adult life in Nashville and Washington, D.C. but he returned to Franklin for good in 1918. Never married, he joined two sisters living at the family home. By 1919, he entered politics, eventually serving nine terms as Franklin's mayor.

Shortly after Park moved back home he decided the house needed updating so he had electricity installed. Alas, modern conveniences did not agree with Park, so he had the wiring ripped right back out. The house was lit by gas and kerosene lamps as long as Park lived. Electricity wasn't installed again until sometime after Park's 1947 death.

The house remained in the Marshall family until 1997, when the last Marshall descendant living in the house passed away.

New owners Fred and Linda Reynolds had their work cut out for them restoring the Marshall House. Nothing had been done to it *for years*. It was derelict inside and out. But it was a house many local people wanted to see, so Fred and Linda decided to have a little pre-renovation house-warming for their friends although they weren't actually living in the house yet.

The guests were wandering through the house, when somebody asked Linda: "Is this house haunted?"

Linda said, "Well if it is, I would like it to be Park Marshall."

As soon as the words were out of her mouth, every light in the house went out. Everyone gasped. The house was pitch black. Park had pulled the plug again.

It's best not to talk about ghosts in the Marshall House unless you really want to hear from one.

Fred, Linda and the guests felt for the light switches, flipped them up and down, but nothing happened. They went down to the basement, flipped the breaker box, and the lights came back on. Nobody brought up ghosts for the rest of the party. It was just too coincidental.

One of the Marshalls had many years before taken his own life in the back yard under one of two large trees. Fred and Linda added onto the house, extending it into the back yard which required cutting down one of the big trees.

One night, Fred said to Linda, "I wonder if this is the tree where Mr. Marshall shot himself."

Again, the house was plunged into darkness. After that the Reynoldses didn't talk about ghosts *or* the Marshalls in the house.

The addition was Fred and Linda's bedroom. One night both woke up to a strange sound coming from the room over their heads. Linda said, groggily, "What is that?"

Fred answered: "It can't be what it sounds like so just go back to sleep!"

What it sounded like, Fred says now, was a very massive piece of furniture being dragged across the floor above them. Problem is, there's no floor up there or anything else for that matter. When they added the room, the attic space above was completely enclosed with no access. There's no way anybody or anything could get in there. But it was apparently moving day in the Fred and Linda's attic that night!

Chapter 4

A Scandal Involving a President and a Woman— No, Not That One

A Franklin man was one of America's most famous men of his time. Today few Americans recognize the name John Henry Eaton; in 1828 everybody knew it, but it wasn't universally praised and admired. In some quarters, he— and his wife—were reviled.

Today also few understand how important Tennessee was to the national political scene in the early to mid 19th century. Granted, no state was more influential than Virginia before the Civil War. But Tennessee, under the political control of Andrew Jackson, ran a close second. Jackson was the first president not to come from one of the original states; he also created what is today the Democratic party.

Brought to national prominent as the "Hero of the Battle of New Orleans," Jackson believed the 1824 election had been stolen from him.

Never first lady because she died before her husband's inauguration, Rachel Donelson Jackson was the love of Andrew's Jackson's life. Jackson would do anything to uphold or avenge her honor, including kill a man in a duel and attempt it several additional times.

And when you're powerful sometimes they want to take you down. They definitely tried to take down Andrew Jackson.

John Eaton's troubles were directly related to Andrew Jackson's and they were in some ways similar.

Jackson married Rachel Donelson Robards in 1791 believing she had been divorced by her abusive husband Lewis.

Two years later Jackson and Rachel learned that Lewis had only just received the divorce and that they had been living together "in sin" for two years. They quickly retook their vows but the damage had been done. Jackson's enemies never failed to draw attention to Rachel's unintended bigamy as a way to denigrate Jackson.

John Henry Eaton was perhaps Andrew Jackson's closest confidante. Eaton and Jackson went way back; both were Tennessee lawyers and Eaton served under Jackson in the War of 1812.

After his election to the presidency in 1828, Jackson had the unenviable task of uniting the warring political factions—old guard vs. new blood, east vs. west—within the country. But Jackson was above all loyal, so he appointed his great friend and biographer John Henry Eaton Secretary of War (today's Secretary of Defense).

John Eaton had just gotten married. The woman he loved, Margaret "Peggy" O'Neale Timberlake, could not have been a worse choice either politically or socially.

Peggy was a beautiful, smart and vivacious woman whom John first met while serving in the U.S. senate ten years before. She was also the daughter of an Irish innkeeper, which did not help her socially in Washington. Gossip about Peggy's teenage romantic escapades was widely known, but by the time John met Peggy, while boarding at her father's inn, she was married to John Timberlake, a naval purser. Timberlake was off at sea for extended periods of time, giving Peggy a lot of free time.

Apparently John and Peggy became good friends and often went riding in carriages together in Timberlake's absence.

In the fall of 1828 Timberlake died off the coast of Spain. The official cause of death was pulmonary disease but the rumor mill suggested he had taken his own life because he was despondent over what Peggy might be doing back in Washington. John Eaton desperately wanted to marry Peggy but was concerned how it would "look." Jackson discouraged delaying the nuptials, saying "If you love Margaret Timberlake go and marry her at once and shut their mouths!"

So he did, on January 1, 1829. It did not shut their mouths, just the opposite. A politician said, "Eaton had just married his mistress—and the mistress of 11 doz. others!" On top of that, it had been just eight months since John Timberlake's death. Societal mourning rules called for widows to reject all social activity for at least one year, stay home, wear black and never smile or laugh (Widowers, on the other hand, only had to wait about five minutes before jumping back into the dating pool).

Peggy Eaton was beautiful, vivacious and was said to have "a form of perfect proportions." Though she rarely got along with women she was able to charm almost any man.

John and Peggy paid a social call on the vice-president's wife, Floride Calhoun, but she would not reciprocate. That snub set the tone. If the other cabinet wives heard that Peggy would be attending a state dinner they would not go. Women crossed the street to avoid speaking to her.

Even Jackson's nephew and personal secretary Andrew Jackson Donelson and his wife Emily would not make nice to the Eatons. Emily said, "His wife is held in too much abhorrence here ever to be noticed or taken into society." The newspapers dubbed it "The Petticoat Affair."

Society's rules were hidebound and immutable. The husbands despaired because they knew that no power on earth could force their wives to associate with another woman they considered a moral inferior. Peggy Eaton certainly fit that category in the eyes of Washington society.

Yet Andrew Jackson remained loyal. He remembered how unfairly people had treated his beloved Rachel, who by now had passed away.

In 1831 two years of contention and animosity came to a head. Secretary of State Martin Van Buren suggested that the entire cabinet resign to promote a fresh start, and he went first, followed by Eaton. The rest followed like dominoes. Andrew Jackson appointed Eaton the governor of the territory of Florida and then the ambassador to Spain. He got them out of Dodge, so to speak.

That worked out well for the Eatons. After John died, he left Peggy a small fortune. She was set for life. Her daughters married well and Peggy finally enjoyed the respect she never had before. It didn't last. At age 59 she married her granddaughter's 19-year-old dance instructor, a recent immigrant from Italy. Five years later he left home with all of her money—and the granddaughter—leaving Peggy bereft and broke. She lived out her years in a home for destitute women.

What a way to end it.

John and Peggy spent a fair amount of time in Franklin after their marriage. In fact, Jackson sent them out to Tennessee in an earlier attempt to "get them out of Dodge"—but it didn't help. Peggy was also in Franklin when a delegation from the Chickasaw nation arrived to meet with Jackson to negotiate a treaty under the Indian Removal Act of 1830. Peggy prepared a barbecue for the visitors and played her piano and sang to them for entertainment after the meal.

People in Franklin liked her. Either they didn't know—or didn't care—about her reputation back in Washington, D.C. John's house on E. Main Street is long gone. Is it possible that Peggy has chosen to spend eternity at the house of a relative at 125 Third Avenue North? A family who lived in the house in the 1950s thinks so.

The house was built about 1818 in the Federal style of architecture. Oral tradition says John Eaton built it for his mother, although now it seems that it was a niece who had it. It has had numerous owners over its almost 200-year history.

By the 1950s, the house was St. Paul's Episcopal Church's rectory. At the time the rector was a single man who lived upstairs. The church rented the downstairs to a young newlywed couple in the church, June and Bill Cameron.

It wasn't long after they moved in that the Camerons began to notice strange sounds—upstairs. After the rector left in the morning, they would hear footsteps up there and what sounded like furniture being dragged across the floor. This happened enough times that the Camerons finally asked the rector about it. He appeared nervous but finally admitted that yes, furniture did move in his absence. In fact, if he moved a chair away from the window in the morning, it would somehow work its way back to the window by the time he got home from work.

Soon it started happening downstairs too: footsteps, doors opening and closing, furniture moving. And as the family expanded, the children began to talk about another person living in the house, a presence. It didn't seem to frighten them.

The Camerons owned a yellow antique lamp that they kept on a table in the living room. Every evening they turned it on and at bedtime turned it off. In the morning when they got up the lamp was turned back on.

Mrs. Cameron remembers: "I'd say, 'Bill, why didn't you turn that lamp off?' and he'd say, 'Well, I did turn it off, you must have turned it back on,' and I'd say, 'No, I didn't, it must have been you . . .' and so on."

So finally they decided the lamp had a defective switch or something, and Bill rewired it. It kept happening. He rewired it again. It kept happening. Finally, they gave up. Whatever, or whoever it was, needed a light on.

This early Federal-style Franklin house has been visited by a
spirit who likes to keep a light on and a chair by the window.

And by this time, the Camerons were pretty well convinced
that Peggy Eaton was the reason.

"She was just lonely . . . and apparently afraid of the dark,"
Mrs. Cameron believes.

Eventually, the family grew out of the house and moved into a brand new house. So was that the end of it? Not by a long shot. She moved with them.

By now the Camerons were so used to having an uninvited guest around the house that they sometimes forgot to warn invited guests of the possibility of an otherworldly visit.

Years passed, and their son Jim went off to college at The University of the South, Sewanee. One Thanksgiving he invited a friend named Steve home for a visit.

After a big noontime meal, the two young men decided to take a nap upstairs in Jim's room. Jim fell asleep and Steve was almost there when something caused him to open his eyes. There at the foot of the bed was the spirit of a woman.

Steve tried wake up Jim but couldn't speak or move for a few moments. Then the spirit floated around to the side of the bed, leaned down and put her hand on the covers next to him. Steve saw the deep impression of her handprint on the comforter. That got his adrenaline pumping. He jumped out of bed and flew downstairs.

"Mrs. Cameron, I've just had an experience!" Steve exclaimed. She could tell because he was as "pale as a ghost."

He described what happened and said he knew it was a woman although he couldn't make out features on her face. He knew because of the old-fashioned clothing she was wearing.

Shortly after that Jim came downstairs and when told about it said he had heard a woman's voice in the room but in his half-sleep it hadn't registered with him. That's when Steve realized why he opened his eyes when he did. He said, "It's come back to me. In my fog of sleep I remember now. She was calling my name, 'Steve, Steve!'" That was enough excitement for Steve. He went back to Sewanee that night.

After college Steve came to Nashville to look for a job and stayed with the Camerons for a month.

"I always told the children to turn the lights off in their rooms when they left, but Steve's light always seemed to be on. So one day I reminded him to please turn off the light," Mrs. Cameron said.

"But Mrs. Cameron, I always turn the light off when I leave in the morning!" Steve insisted.

Somebody is afraid of the dark . . .

Mrs. Cameron is now a widow and lives alone. She doesn't hear from Peggy Eaton these days.

"She seems mostly to like being around children, where there's a lot of activity and noise. It's really quiet around my house. In fact, years ago, she moved in with my son Michael and his family."

Michael's wife Jeri first experienced Peggy shortly after they married.

"I woke up in the morning and reached for my glasses beside the bed. They had been dismantled. The screws were out of the earpieces. All the parts were there but I had to put them back together," said Jeri.

Jeri thinks that Peggy was checking her tolerance level. "She wanted to see what kind of person I was going to be with Michael's children. She wanted to make sure I would treat the children well. She was very protective of the children."

Remember the yellow antique lamp that kept turning itself on in the night? Now Jeri and Michael have it. One Easter their extended families were there for dinner. Afterwards, Jeri started talking about Peggy.

"My dad didn't like this and said, 'Stop talking about it. I hate it when you bring this up. It's weird!' At that, the lamp got noticeably brighter. My sister said, 'How did you do that?!' and walked over to the lamp," Jeri recalled.

"The lamp started shaking like we were having an earthquake. My sister's eyes were as big as saucers. My dad said, 'I said to stop talking about it!'"

"Later my mom said she had felt a cold breeze blow through the room when I started talking about her."

Sounds like Peggy wanted to hear what they were saying about her and just didn't like being described as "weird."

Over the years Jeri had numerous encounters with Peggy.

"Once I heard somebody falling down the stairs, boomba, boomba, just like it sounds. I heard someone walk into the bedroom when I was sitting at my makeup mirror. Once when

Michael was out of town I felt hands patting around the bed. One night we heard my jewelry box sliding across our oak dresser."

Back in college, long before Jeri met Michael, she studied Peggy Eaton and "The Eaton Affair" in history class.

"The professor talked about Peggy supposedly being Andrew Jackson's mistress. I wrote a paper called "The Defense of Peggy Eaton" to tell the truth about it. I really like Peggy. I've never seen her but I wish I would."

Jeri doesn't claim to fully understand ghosts and spirits, but believes that "souls at unrest will not move on. I totally understand why she was stuck," she said.

Jeri and Michael's children are grown and gone. Like Michael's parents before him, they don't hear from Peggy anymore, and Jeri says that "if she's moved on and found contentment, good for her."

Back to 125 Third Avenue North.

The church sold the house to a woman who then sold to the firm of lawyers there today. They're not around much at night and have nothing to report. But shortly after they moved in a woman from Kentucky came in, spoke to the receptionist and then conferred with one of the lawyers.

The next day she phoned the office, and asked the receptionist, "Do you know you have a ghost in your building?"

Peggy dictated an autobiography in 1873 that was first published almost 50 years after her death, in 1932. About life after the third marriage ended, she wrote, "Youth and bloom were gone, property was swept away, my husband had forsaken me, and old age was coming, and there was nothing left but God . . ."

"Oh, we've heard the stories about a woman who haunted this building years ago," the receptionist told her. "But nobody here has ever seen or heard anything."

"Well, I have. Yesterday when I walked in the door, she was standing at the top of the stairs."

Peggy has also visited at the house called Cherry Manor on the corner of Third Avenue and Bridge Street. Jim Short, who was living there in the early 1980s, was awakened one night by what he describes as a "chill blast of air."

"It was the middle of summer and we were doing renovations on the house. There was no electricity working at the time and it was very hot," Jim said. "It got very cold, and I woke up and saw a gray swirling misty image above me, nose to nose with me. It was the spirit of a woman."

Next thing Jim knew, he was standing in the middle of Third Avenue, thinking, "What the hell was that?"

Once in the middle of the night his step-daughter got up to get a drink of water from the kitchen. She came through the den and discovered the spirit a woman in a long gown on the landing of the staircase. She ran back to rouse her husband but by the time they got back the spirit had disappeared.

So, Peggy Eaton gets around . . . but didn't she always get around? At least that was the perception, and doesn't perception become reality?

In the 20th century Peggy Eaton became a cautionary tale for young Franklin women. One middle-aged tour guest, a Franklin native, reminisced about her wild teenage years. "I was going out, breaking curfew, carousing, doing all the things I wasn't supposed to be doing. Nothing my mother did or said stopped me, until one day, she took me aside, and said ominously, 'If you don't stop what you're doing, you're going to end up just like Peggy Eaton, sentenced to roam Third Avenue for all eternity!' I didn't want that, so I straightened right up!"

Chapter 5

It Was Not a Bed of Roses

The Bennett House was a well-known Franklin recording studio for many years. Read CD liner notes of many well-known pop and country artists and you often find recordings made at The Bennett House, Franklin, Tennessee. That Bennett House is located on Fourth Avenue North. Reportedly, that Bennett House is haunted.

But that's not the Bennett House we're talking about. We're talking about the Bennett House on Third Avenue North.

The story starts with a family named Glass, who arrived in Williamson County sometime before 1815. Samuel Fielding Glass was a wealthy planter and also owned a hat factory in town. He died in 1859 leaving three surviving children, including his namesake, Samuel Fielding Glass, Jr.

The son was determined to increase his family's holdings. In 1865 he declared that he wanted to own everything currently belonging to the two wealthiest families in town. Those families were the McGavocks and Perkinses. He almost succeeded, buying up acres and acres of the best farmland in Williamson County from these families.

Sam married Agnes Hunter. The marriage produced two sons, William and David, and two daughters, Corinne and Laura. This story is about Laura.

It had been Sam Glass's practice to give each child a large tract of land. They would inherit it eventually anyway and this would give them a means of support starting out in life. Laura's property was prime farmland five miles west of town on the West Harpeth River. So when she married her distant cousin Emmett Bennett in 1881, Emmett gave up the practice of law to work the farm. However, the couple lived in town in a large Victorian house on Third Avenue North.

After eight years, during which their only child, a daughter named Agnes was born, things turned sour between Emmett and the Glass family.

In the later court cases, and there were three not including appeals, what's clear is that Emmett did not like farming. He said he could not make the farm pay. What's also clear is that Sam's ego equaled the size of his fortune and tact and diplomacy were not his strong suits. He told his son-in-law that he was stupid, in so many words. He also meddled. When Emmett sold Laura's horse because he believed it to be unsafe, Sam bought it back for Laura. Eventually Sam and Emmett stopped speaking.

In February 1889 Laura deeded her property back to her father. Shortly after that, Laura went with her parents to Nashville to consult a lawyer. She came back to Franklin and immediately moved out of her house and into her parents'. Laura and Emmett never lived together as husband and wife again. Then her father deeded the property back to her.

Emmett sued his father-in-law for an old cause of action called alienation of affection. What Emmett had to prove was that Sam used property to gain influence over Laura in an attempt to destroy the marriage.

Emmett proved it. The testimony showed, and the jury believed, that Sam had asked for the property back (and the deed confirms that fact), and told Laura that she could have it back if she left Emmett. The jury awarded Emmett $10,000. Sam was so enraged after the verdict that he ripped off all his clothing and jumped in the Harpeth River, where he flailed around until someone fished him out. He was never the same again, and died a few years later.

Emmett divorced Laura and moved away, and Laura and Agnes lived in the house on Third Avenue. Laura never remarried. The stigma of divorce in those days would have made her ineligible to many men, and maybe she just didn't want to remarry. We just don't know. The couple's bed was taken to the attic for storage and Laura slept in a different bed. After Laura died, Miss Agnes Bennett, as she was known to all, lived there alone.

After Miss Agnes died in 1977 the house and its contents sold. At some point, Jim Short (Remember him from the last chapter? Peggy visited him at Cherry Manor in the middle of the night.) purchased Laura and Emmett's bed for Cherry Manor.

The Short family, who lived there from 1972 until 2000, had other strange experiences that sound very unlike our amiable but lonely Peggy Eaton. Six porcelain plates that had been placed carefully for display on the mantel had crashed to the floor, while other objects in front of them had not moved. Silk flowers in a large vase ended up on the floor while the vase stayed upright. A pair of scissors flew across the room. Peggy never did anything malicious or violent. So what was this all about?

Now business offices, Cherry Manor has been a private home over the years as well as a combination nursing home/funeral parlor, which had to be somewhat demoralizing for the residents.

People on tour have heard knocking, banging, crashing and one man even claimed to see a woman's face looking out one of the front windows, a face reflecting "hate, spite and rage. And that woman telling stories about me needs to stop!" (That would be me . . .)

Cherry Manor is the house on the tour that gets the most reaction from guests. Some complain of weird, creepy feelings. One man got the willies—on steroids.

Gary Harmon stood on the street in front of Cherry Manor listening to my tour on an early summer night in 2003. He suddenly felt sick to his stomach. Not a nagging ache, but a full-on, gut-busting pain that he began to think was food poisoning. He clutched his stomach and walked back the direction we had come, toward Main Street. As soon as he crossed the property line to the next house the pain disappeared. So he returned to Cherry Manor, and just as fast the pain returned. This time he was convinced it was food poisoning and he needed help fast. So he enlisted his friend David Garrett, who accompanied him on the tour, to help him find a bathroom. As soon as they passed the property line the pain disappeared. He rejoined the tour at the next stop.

At the end of the tour, Gary sought me out to explain his behavior. I said, "How odd, what do you think it was?"

"There's an evil spirit in that house," Gary said. As I stared wide-eyed he explained that he has the "burden" of clairvoyance, and has since early childhood. Some people call it a gift; sometimes he wishes it would just go away.

"I usually get a nervous stomach, or the hair on my arms or the back of my neck will stand up. This was the worst feeling I've ever had and I know what it means."

"Oh!" I said, "Do you think it's Peggy and she's mad at me?"

"No, she's there too, but she's benign. It's this other one . . . not nice."

Vivian and David Garrett, Gary Harmon's friends, purchased Laurel Hill, an 1830s plantation house about five miles south of Franklin on Columbia Pike in 2003.

Gary and his wife Katherine visited David and Vivian in late 2007. They were sitting downstairs when David told Gary that he had bought a beautifully carved Eastlake-style bed from Cherry Manor for the guest bedroom.

Gary, shocked, said, "I can't believe you brought this bed from that house into your home!"

David asked Gary to use his powers to tell him about the bed.

"I started walking around the bed. I didn't know anything about it," Gary said.

After a few minutes, Gary said, "I told him there was a couple who had bought it and they didn't stay together. The wife left the husband. She wasn't happy with the husband. He couldn't satisfy her. It's the husband who haunts the bed."

So far, so good. That could be Emmett Bennett. From the court records, he seemed pretty ticked off most of the time.

Then Gary decided to "provoke" the ghost. He belittled him, casting aspersions upon his manhood. A blast of air, "like from a blow dryer but room temperature," hit Gary and David. Later they tried to recreate the blast of air from the same location in the room but couldn't.

This beautiful bed has a checkered history. Once the marriage bed of Emmett and Laura Bennett, the bed is believed to be haunted by the husband.

Gary continued to provoke the ghost. This time he felt a tap on his shoulder, then finally three tugs on his belt loop.

That never happened before. They got spooked and quit.

Gary has never slept in the bed and never will, but others have.

A young friend of the Garretts reported having been thrown around the bed and then finally pitched out of it. A mother and daughter spent an eventful night on the bed. The mother sensed someone touching her all night and the daughter felt someone lying on top of her.

Not everyone had a disagreeable experience, but the Garretts got rid of the bed. They just wanted it—and the ghost that accompanied it—out!

Chapter 6

The Party House

If you ask most people to define a townhouse, they'll describe it as one of a row of narrow two or three story apartments of condominiums sharing common side walls, often sited up close to city sidewalks. In fact, visitors point to Franklin's elegant and high-end Brownstones, located on Second Avenue South and Church Street, and ask me, "Are those townhouses old?" No, they're not. They replaced a parking lot that replaced worker housing for a mill that once stood on First Avenue. (The location itself had an evocative name: Bucket of Blood. About 1910 a man named Pig Hogue (if your last name is Hogue, isn't "Pig" just the perfect nickname) was stabbed and reportedly bled so much it filled a bucket. But the developer wisely chose to name these dwellings "The Brownstones" over the historically accurate Bucket of Blood.)

But there's another definition for town house, and it's actually the original definition: a house in town owned by a family whose main residence was in the country.

Clouston Hall after a light snowfall in 2011

Clouston Hall, diagonally across the street from the Brownstones, served this purpose for the Clouston family in the early 19ᵗʰ century. In Texas they call them "Sunday Houses" because families coming to town to attend church needed lodging.

Clouston Hall might be better described as a "Saturday House" because social gatherings, parties and political events all took place there. All three Tennessee U.S. Presidents—Jackson, Polk and Andrew Johnson—reportedly visited the house. The big folding doors separating the parlors downstairs could be opened into one big room to accommodate Christmas celebrations, birthday parties, weddings and funerals.

Joseph Reiff, the architect who designed and rebuilt the current Hermitage for Andrew Jackson after his first house burned, also designed Clouston Hall. This Federal style home is typical in that its front windows are in three parts separated by a pilaster (flat column) and arranged symmetrically around the center doorway, which has divided sidelights (or windows) and a fanlight atop the door. Inside are original pine and poplar floors, 15-foot ceilings, and hand-carved buttonhole moldings, mantels and doors.

Its elegant, tranquil appearance notwithstanding, Clouston Hall has quite a tumultuous history. Edward Clouston's daughter committed suicide by hanging herself from the upstairs banister on the eve of her wedding. Later, Clouston lost a lawsuit and was forced to forfeit his home. After the Battle of Franklin, the house was one of 44 field hospitals for the wounded, and blood of the soldiers treated there still stains the heart pine floors by a front downstairs window. One soldier brought to the house had his jaw shot away, and he slowly starved to death because he couldn't take in nourishment. The center hall bears the scar of a 3-lb. cannonball that tore through the roof during the Battle of Franklin.

Dr. D.B. Cliffe owned the house from 1920-40, then sold it after he lost his medical license for narcotics violations.

In the 20th century owner Bunn Gray's activities brought the house attention as he threw non-stop parties for his large circle of friends and admirers.

Walter Bunn Gray, a Fayetteville, Tennessee native, moved to Franklin as a child. At an early age he displayed talent as a painter, winning national contests as young as age four. He graduated from Florida State University and moved first to Miami, then New York City in the early 1960s where he had gallery showings within six weeks of arriving. He achieved some celebrity and fell in with the Andy Warhol-art crowd. Missing

Tennessee, Bunn decided to move back home in 1964, fortuitous timing for Clouston Hall, which was threatened with demolition to make way for a gas station. Bunn paid $13,000 for the house, moved in, and lived there for the next 38 years.

Alternatively described as flamboyant and colorful, Bunn made sure there was never a dull moment at 202 2nd Avenue. When the doorbell rang, Bunn jumped from his chair, flapped his arms like wings, and marched to the door, ready for anything.

Bunn Gray saved Clouston Hall from the wrecking ball in 1964 and lived in the house until he died in 2002. He imbued the house with an "aura and mystique" as recalled by one of his many friends.

"Everybody loved Bunn," said friend Rusty Womack. "You never knew who you were going to run into there. It was kind of like a frat house atmosphere, but more of a family atmosphere. All day long people were in and out. When he was painting, there was a lot of energy there. With Bunn they broke the mold. He was a special friend and so good-hearted."

At some point Bunn needed help making ends meet, so he began to take in boarders. The house has four main rooms downstairs all of which were rented out. One day someone noticed a foul odor coming from one of the rooms. They broke in and found the rapidly decaying body of a man, who, it was determined, had died accidentally. Let's just say that there was rope involved.

After Bunn died, Rusty Womack acquired it with the unspoken commitment that he would restore it. Rusty put his heart and soul into it, and returned the house to its former glory. Until 2010 the house was used for offices, but that all changed when Gallery 202 opened in 2010.

History Embraces Art

Gallery 202 has quickly become the premier fine art gallery in Franklin, featuring the paintings, sculpture and jewelry of 45 artists from across the nation. Owner and artist-in-residence Kelly Harwood and gallery manager Jim McReynolds have created a welcoming environment for art aficionados and visitors I tour through the house, narrating its history, pointing out architectural details—and the bloodstains and cannonball scar. It's a great addition to my tour, and access to the building is truly appreciated by visitors. I've said to Kelly and Jim many times that I cannot imagine a better use for Clouston Hall than as this art gallery (unless I could move in, that is).

Kelly Harwood indicates the spot where Elizabeth Clouston unequivocally and irrevocably broke her engagement.

Visitors come to Gallery 202 for the history and the art, and the good ole Southern hospitality extended by Kelly and Jim. Others find all that, and something else.

One evening shortly after the gallery opened, Kelly hosted a dinner party in the house. He opened the door as guests began arriving. A woman came to the door, as Kelly greeted her, saying, "Welcome to Clouston Hall."

The woman stood at the threshold, gazing expectantly into the interior of the house and said, "I can't come in until I'm welcome."

Kelly smiled, "It's my house. You're welcome to come in."

The woman replied, "Not you, *them.*"

A few seconds passed, and the woman slowly entered the building. She pointed to the center hall, near the staircase, and said, "She's swinging," as she waved her arms back and forth to demonstrate what she was "seeing." Then she pointed to the dining room, and described a row of soldiers standing with their backs to the wall. She said the soldiers were at guard, protecting the house. She assured Kelly were no "bad feelings" associated with the house.

This was Kelly's first inkling that when he bought the house it came with unseen assets.

One snowy winter day, Jim and Kelly were both in the building, working on various projects. Kelly heard the sounds of laughter coming from the entrance with voices calling out, "Here! c'mon, run, run!" It sounded like children playing and Kelly figured they'd come to scoop up snow for snowballs.

"There goes my chance for a photo of the building with fresh snow," Kelly mused.

He went to the front to look out the windows, and not only were there no children, there were no footprints of children (or anyone else) in the snow. He told Jim, who was in the back, and Jim told him, "I hear that all the time."

Jim said he often hears children playing, laughing, running, giggling, calling out. Once he made out the name "Kevin." It made Kelly realize he'd heard what sounded like someone whistling while he was painting alone one day.

Jim recalled an interesting visit from a plumber.

"I was writing a check to pay him, when we both heard the door from the dining room into the butler's pantry open, creaking the way it usually does. And of course, there was no one there."

"You've got them too," said the plumber, and he went on to describe numerous service calls to downtown houses and the strange experiences he'd had, especially, he said, *under* houses.

One day he and his helper, his son, were working under a house, with a utility light for illumination. The son left the crawl space to retrieve something from the truck, so the plumber decided to turn off the light. As soon as he did he felt a strong presence coming toward him. He turned the light back on, and the feeling ended. He turned it off again, and the presence returned. He turned the light back on and left it on.

Clouston Hall's basement is unfinished—in fact the ceiling height is just 6 ft. There's a narrow opening from the main room into another room that would be difficult to squeeze through. Kelly once stuck his head through the opening to see what was there, and the hair stood up on the back of his neck. He's heard rumors that there were bodies there after the Battle of Franklin.

During the Bunn Gray years, one houseguest woke up in the middle of the night to find the ethereal form of a woman sitting on the edge of his bed. He leapt from bed and ran outside shrieking at the top of his lungs. He phoned the next day and asked Bunn to place his belonging on the sidewalk. Bunn asked why he'd left so abruptly. When the guest related his experience, Bunn told him, "Oh, that's just Miss Ninny."

*Ninny Nichols Cliffe was an "unreconstructed Confederate"
although she later married into a staunch Union family.*

Cornelia "Ninny" Nichols Cliffe was a fervent Confederate partisan about whom stories are legion in Franklin. As the Union army approached Franklin in 1862, she spread hot burning coals from her fireplace over the boards of the bridge crossing the Harpeth River in an attempt to burn it down, to keep the Yankees out.

It didn't keep them out—they entered Franklin and began the three-year military occupation—and in fact, that the bridge was impassable by wagons and cannons is the reason there was a battle fought in Franklin. (See chapter 9).

St Andrews Bay News, St Andrews, Florida, Tuesday, Dec 18, 1928
Noted Woman of Old South Passes Away

Old residents of St Andrews, *who recall Dr. Daniel B Cliffe, of* Franklin, Tenn., for many years a regular visitor to St Andrews each year during tarpon fishing season, will learn with regret of the death of his mother, Mrs. Cornelia N Cliffe, which occurred at Dr. Cliffe's home in Franklin, on December 9.

Mrs. Cliffe, the wife of a captain in the Union army during the Civil War, was conspicuous for her devotion to the "lost cause", and on one occasion, with only the aid of an old man, faced the fire of a Union battery to burn the Nashville bridge and halt for a time the Federal army advancing on Franklin.

After the battle at Franklin, she was among the first on the field to minister to the wounded Confederates, and her home was converted into a hospital.

After the war, Mrs. Cliffe made the first robes for the Ku Klux Klan in Williamson County, Tennessee, and when the organization was disbanded, the robes were sent to her to be destroyed.

Mrs. Cliffe was daughter of John Nichols, a prominent North Carolinian. While her husband wore the Union blue, all of her brothers served the South under the Stars and Bars.

During the Battle of Franklin, a Union officer reportedly approached her house, attempting to break in. Ninny found her daddy's revolver, pointed it at him, and shot. The gun misfired badly, severing her thumb. Forever after Ninny wore a pair of gloves with fabric stuffed into the thumb. After the war, she married a young Union captain, a West Point graduate named James B. Cliffe. When her friends asked her why she'd married a Yankee, she replied that if she wanted to get married she had to— all the Confederate boys were dead.

Bunn always believed it was Miss Ninny who approached male houseguests in the middle of the night. For one thing, although Clouston Hall was never her primary residence, the house belonged to her son, and, after Miss Ninny's husband died, she moved in with her son and died in the house. For another, he said several observers pointed out that the spirit seemed to be wearing gloves. Yep, it all fit.

Bunn had a fascination with the number 2, as shown in his painting here. The urn in front of the piece contains Bunn's ashes.

Rusty Womack spent many days and evenings in the house during the restoration process, both alone and with other workers. A large secretary that had belonged to Bunn remained in the house during that time.

"We had to keep moving it around to get it out of the way, and one day someone moved it to the center hall where, when you'd open the front door, it banged against the secretary, "Rusty relates.

"So one evening I moved it myself enough so that the door wouldn't hit it. It was a big heavy thing. It took a lot of effort. Then I locked up and left. When I came back an hour later after eating dinner, and opened the door, it banged into that secretary. It had moved."

"It was the only thing that gave me pause. It happened, and I can't explain it. I was flabbergasted."

Rusty was sorry to sell the house, but he's glad it's an art gallery and open to the public.

Bunn's ashes were returned to Clouston Hall by a friend after Gallery 202 opened.

Rusty reflects, "Bunn's back, and he's where he needs to be. He would be so glad that the house is open to the public. He would want everyone to enjoy it."

Chapter 7

A Spirited Main Street

Franklin's Main Street of today is a hip and happenin' place. Chic clothing boutiques, specialty shops selling chocolate, cupcakes, African art and gardening items, restaurants ranging from fine dining to meat 'n three, trendy stores, a spa and a bookstore, all cater to well-heeled locals and visitors. Main Street also has its churches, banks, lawyers' offices and Franklin City Hall.

It's a real town. Nonetheless, it's a very different town than it was even 25 years ago.

For most of its 212 year existence (as of 2011), Franklin was known as a rough place where dangerous things could happen. Recently, two women in town for a funeral came on my daytime tour.

They told their local relatives they were taking a Main Street tour at 10:00 a.m. on a Saturday morning in March. Their relatives' response: "Are you sure it's safe?"

These relatives, who were born and grew up in Franklin in the mid-20th Century, knew that is that it *wasn't* always safe in

Franklin. Murders occurred in downtown Franklin with surprising regularity. Rowdy beer joints and honky-tonks attracted toughs from all over the area. Prostitution was commonplace. Certain alleys were not safe to walk through.

People from out of town can hardly believe it because today Franklin's authentic Main Street looks like Disney World's ersatz Main Street.

Trust me. I've done the research. And sometimes when murders take place, spirits are left behind.

Historically, Main Street was the commercial mecca for Franklin and the outlying areas—on Saturday the streets and shops were packed with town and country folk. Today Franklin is a destination for visitors from all over the world who crowd the downtown shops and restaurants.

He Hadn't Moved On

The oldest building still standing on the square is called the Maury-Darby building and it dates back to 1813. Originally a doctor's office, by the 1930s the building was an apartment building called Cochrane Flats.

If you hear a loud thud upstairs in this building, don't bother to investigate.

A couple named Gladys and Everett Reed were living there in December 1935 with Gladys's two children from her first marriage. One day when Everett and the children were away from home, Gladys's first husband Fred Beard came to the apartment, shot Gladys twice and then himself. *Thud!* His body fell to the floor. He left a note that said, "Please just bury me next to my mama." When the bodies were found, nothing else was disturbed or out of order.

Now the building is a law office. A secretary was working there alone once. When she went out to lunch she locked the door and then of course unlocked it to get back in. After a short time she heard footsteps moving around upstairs, and then what sounded like something very heavy dropping to the floor. *Thud!*

She thought one of the lawyers had come in while she was at lunch so she called out. No one answered. After about 20 minutes of working up her courage to check it out, she finally went upstairs. There was no sign of anything having fallen. Nothing was disturbed or out of order. The secretary doesn't like to be alone in the building anymore.

This Bank Wasn't Too Big To Fail

The building next door originally housed the National Bank of Franklin. One day in 1926, whispers went through town that the National Bank of Franklin was in trouble. A native Franklinite recalls his mother saying she was at the grocery store with her mother when the rumor floated around that the bank had failed. The woman behind her in line fainted.

Pre-FDIC, a bank failure meant depositors were busted. It turned out that the bank's operators, a father and son, had looted the bank, cooking the books and pilfering valuables out of depositors' safe deposit boxes. Mayor Park Marshall was on the board of directors and the City of Franklin's payroll was on deposit. Unfortunately, in the booming 1920s, corporate oversight was overlooked. This may sound similar to a recent decade of the modern era.

The National Bank of Franklin was not a safe place to keep your money and valuables back in the 1920s.

Now the building is a lawyer's office. In recent years, the folks working there profess not to believe in ghosts. However, they can't explain:

- Lights starting out very low and then gradually building up to full brightness
- Ditto the ceiling fan
- Footsteps upstairs when no one's there

Once, one of the lawyers working alone at night heard footsteps in the outer office. She called out, no one answered, so she pulled out her gun and went out to investigate. As soon as she walked into the outer office, a sheaf of papers on the desk flew up into the air, although the room was as still as a morgue. Apparently someone is still messing with the books.

Landmark's the Spot

Sometimes, it's really tough to identify the spirit that's hanging around a particular building. Take a place like Landmark Booksellers, for example. Landmark's building, the oldest commercial building in town, has had so many uses over time that it's difficult to pin down.

The building at 114 E. Main Street has been dated definitively back to 1825 but recent research indicates it may have been built around 1808. If that's the case the building stands as the earliest example of Greek Revival architecture west of the Allegheny Mountains. Oral tradition says that it was from a building at that location that Andrew Jackson paid his troops after marching up the Natchez Trace during the War of 1812.

The first unambiguous use of the present structure was as the company store for a flour and cotton mill located on East Margin Street (now First Avenue).

It was also a field hospital after the Battle of Franklin for both Union and Confederate soldiers. The brother of a soldier who died in the building later became governor of Tennessee.

Old Factory Store on East Main Street

Tom Lawrence of radio station WAKM saw a woman dressed in black on the balcony of this building early one morning—and nobody lives here.

After the war it was sold and its connection to the mill was severed. Jeremiah Shea purchased it in 1884, and it remained in the Shea family until the 1940s as a grocery store. Since then it has been a restaurant (Dotson's, which moved down the street), and an antiques and furniture repair shop.

In the 21st century, the building held a jewelry store on the first floor and a business called Old Town Lending on the second.

An employee at the jewelry store was surprised when a woman dropped in one day and asked, "Have you met the ghost yet?"

She hadn't.

The visitor said that she had worked in the building "sometime after WWII" and quit because she was sick of the ghost. She didn't give much detail but did say the ghost only came out after 5 p.m.

Upstairs the Old Town Lending folks *had* met the ghost. In fact, J.D. Ryan, who worked upstairs, kept a diary of the strange occurrences:

> *7/19/04 —Strange observation. I came into the office early this morning. As I walked by [other employee's] office, I noticed the blinds were half up and not even. I walked into his office to adjust the blinds and noticed two of the casters were off of his chair. I wondered what he had been doing, but I just assumed that he had done it on purpose. I could only imagine that he was trying to lean back more than the chair's mechanism would allow. I forgot to mention it to [him] that day. To be honest, I don't know if I saw him today."*

> *7/20/04 — All seemed normal this morning, however a strange tale to tell. About mid morning, Julia decided to use [other employee's] office to work on an upcoming ad. I heard her making a lot of noise and decided to offer assistance. As I entered the room I asked if she needed any help. She responded by saying that three of the casters had come off of [his] chair. I asked, 'How many?' She said, 'Three.' I told her the story from the day before. We decided to ask [him] if he had removed the wheels for any reason. He said without hesitation, 'NO, NOT ME.'*

> *Later that afternoon, Julia and I were working on loan documentation and heard the motion alarm. We looked at each*

other and decided to check it out. As we walked down the hall, past the alarm it sounded again (meaning it was working). We checked the bathroom, lobby, and the stair way. Let me not forget to mention that before we decided to investigate, we heard water running at a faucet. When I checked the sinks, they were dry.

7/30/04 – Approximately 10:30 pm, we, the three of us were working late. We had just installed a software package for producing and tracking loan documents. We were loading existing loans onto the system and ran into a problem. [Other employee] decided he was going home. Julia and I resolved to figure out the problem on our own. She was opposite of me on the same end of my desk. We were facing each other, trying to manually calculate loan amortizations. I was using my 10 key calculator, when all of a sudden my desk reference book and a lamp on the other end of my desk fell off of my desk. By the way, my desk is six feet wide and three feet front to back. The book went first. Being heavy, it made a loud noise. It startled me and I looked immediately in that direction to watch the lamp move off of the table and fall. We looked at each other in amazement. Both concluded that it had to be a spirit of some sort. We managed to stay until around 11:30 pm.

8/3/04 – Today yet another strange tale to tell. I don't remember the exact time but it was close to mid-day. Julia mentioned that we had not heard from the ghost in a while. At that time, there were four loud knocks. I couldn't tell where it came from, but we looked at each other and went to the door; there was no one there. Later that afternoon, Jan from downstairs at the jewelry store came up to see my lamp and book. She told the three of us that one day a lady came into the jewelry store to tell her of her experiences. It seems the lady had *worked upstairs a few years ago. Long and short, she had to quit because of a ghost. She indicated it was a male, but gave no explanation.*

---*J.D. Ryan*

Current building owners and bookstore proprietors Carol and Joel Tomlin have not sensed a ghost in the building (although a stepladder seems to move around on its own), but the same cannot be said for their friend and occasional employee Cathy Clarkson.

"I was the last one in the store one day about 5:30 p.m.," Cathy remembers. "I had set the alarm and turned out all the lights and gotten all my stuff. I went outside and turned and locked the door. Then I noticed the sign."

The sign is a sandwich board-type sign that sits out on the sidewalk all day. The city requires it be brought in at night.

Cathy thought, "Well, I've got to bring the sign in." So she put her stuff down, grabbed the handle on the sign and began to wheel it back to the door which she unlocked and opened.

"As soon as I opened the door, an awful groaning sound poured forth from the back of the building where the stairs are. I knew what it was. It was the ghost," Cathy said.

"So I spoke into the building. I said, 'I'm just going to be a second. I have to bring the sign in and then I'll leave and you can have your building back.'"

The building now housing Landmark Booksellers has such a long history that it's difficult to determine who just can't let go of it in the afterlife.

The sound immediately ceased. Cathy wheeled in the sign, turned around and left.

Cathy has heard footsteps walking around on the second floor and stairs at times, as has Joel's son, who had his office in the building for a time.

At a Landmark book signing, two guests who had been browsing upstairs came down to report to Joel that a book had flown off its shelf and landed across the room, right in front of them.

But who is this ghost with the good pitching arm? Nobody knows for sure who it is or even its gender. J.D. suggested a male, perhaps a Civil War soldier, while Cathy always felt it was a female, although she says, "I don't know why."

Tom Lawrence agrees with Cathy, because he saw the spirit.

The long-time voice of AM 1510, WAKM, Tom keeps early hours, usually arriving at the station before 4 a.m. One ordinary Tuesday morning several years ago he drove as usual on Main Street north to the station on Mallory Station Lane. At that hour of the morning, Franklin's streets are deserted.

"I came around the square, toward Second Avenue. I looked at the building that was then Old Town Lending. I had always admired the balcony and generally looked at it," Tom recalled.

"I saw a figure standing on the balcony. There was a lady standing there in black. I drove to the red light at First Avenue, rolled down my window and stuck my head out to look back, but she was gone.

"I thought I better call J. D. and tell him someone was standing on his balcony. I ran into him a few days later and told him about it. He told me, 'We are very familiar with her.'"

From the looks of this early 20ᵗʰ century postcard, not much has changed on Franklin's Main Street.

Chapter 8

No Place on Earth They'd Rather Be

What do a warehouse and a mansion on South Margin Street in Franklin have in common? Not much except their owners loved their buildings so much they never wanted to leave.

Harris owned an antiques store in an old warehouse building at 125 S. Margin Street in downtown Franklin in the 1960s-70s. He was a retired school superintendent from Mississippi but given a choice where to hang out in the afterlife, he picked Franklin.

After Harris died in 1970s, the building changed hands several times and went through several incarnations. Today it houses J.J. Ashley's furniture and décor. Marianne DeMeyers, who opened Tin Cottage in the rear of the building in 1999, was puzzled by little "yipping" noises she heard in the store. Marianne thought maybe birds had roosted under the eaves or perhaps rats were nesting in the attic. She and an employee thoroughly searched the attic but could never find any sign of infestation.

Had that been the extent of it, Marianne might not have thought much about it. It wasn't until a customer named Sue did something completely uncharacteristic that Marianne realized something was up.

Sue was a regular who would come in at least once a week to hang around the store and chat. She was familiar with the place because she had worked for Harris back in the 1960s in his antique store.

"One day, right in the middle of our conversation, Sue turned as white as a sheet and said 'I'm leaving, I'm leaving!'" said Marianne. "She left abruptly. It was very strange."

This humble but useful building appears to be the afterlife destination of choice for one former Franklin antiques dealer.

And she didn't come back. Several weeks went by and Sue didn't show up, so Marianne became concerned.

"I finally called her, and her husband answered the phone. She wouldn't or couldn't talk to me that day but called me back the next day. Sue said, 'I don't want you to think I'm crazy but I left suddenly because I saw Harris standing behind you.'"

She described him as an outgoing, portly gentleman with a short beard and a long overcoat. Even in the afterlife, Sue had no trouble recognizing him.

Sue had called Harris's widow, who had moved back to Mississippi, to tell her about seeing Harris in the store. Harris's wife giggled and said, "If he's anywhere on earth, he's at that store. It was his absolute favorite place."

Sue also told Marianne that Harris owned a miniature pinscher that he brought to the store. Harris would talk to the dog and the dog would answer by yipping. Voila! That explained the sound.

Harris had very definite taste in music, and it didn't always match Marianne's.

"He loved old jazz and the music of Frank Sinatra and Nat King Cole. Anything by [jazz pianist] Beegie Adair," Marianne said. "But when we played something on the radio or stereo he didn't like, you could actually see the dial move as he turned it down.

"He was all about customer service. If he thought music like rap or reggae or rock might be offensive to a customer, he would turn it down when someone walked in."

Marianne and her employees could communicate with Harris, too. They would speak aloud to Harris and Harris would reply by moving objects around the store.

"He would sort of throw or drop things, but never anything heavy," Marianne recalls. "And it was often late at night when it happened and I thought he was encouraging me to go home to my family."

She sometimes felt an oppressive presence while working late at night. "It was like something pressing down on my back. I would say to Harris, 'Alright, I know you want me to go home!'"

Meanwhile, Marianne moved her business next door to a little restored house at 123 S. Margin Street. "Harris liked me, and followed me there," Marianne reports.

Gallery 202's Kelly Harwood, who at the time worked at the building next door, came over to tell Marianne he'd come across a strange man in the tool room. "I saw him!" Kelly said, white as a sheet. He described him as an older man with a beard and gave other details such as the big overcoat.

"The description fit Harris to a T," Marianne said.

A few years later Marianne closed Tin Cottage and then opened a new business called Philanthropy on Main Street. And guess what? Harris followed her there.

"I think he likes having someone to talk to and communicate with," said Marianne, who describes herself as a "ghost talker," a trait she inherited from her Cherokee grandmother.

Occasionally Harris tags along with Marianne in her car. "One day I was playing a big rockin' Toby Mac song, and Harris turned it down. I said, 'For crying out loud, Harris, he's a Christian artist!'"

Meanwhile, two blocks east on South Margin Street is another building much loved from beyond. In contrast o the simple and rustic utilitarian old warehouse Harris loved is the splendid Abbey Leix mansion.

Abbey Leix, O'More College of Design's main building at 423 South Margin, is located on property once owned by a Professor McNutt and his wife. The location, at the intersection of S. Margin, Fifth Avenue South and Lewisburg Avenue was the site of what is sometimes called the first Battle of Franklin fought on April 10, 1863. The battle resulted in a Union victory and 237 total casualties. Bodies of men and horses were scattered on the front lawn of the house. The battle was a mere prelude to the bloody and dramatic Battle of Franklin 18 months later, where nearly 10,000 soldiers were killed, wounded or captured and a town was forever scarred by one terrifying and gruesome day.

Four cannons placed on a slight elevation called Berry Circle next to the McNutt house blasted a great rain of fire upon the men attacking on the eastern flank of the battlefield. This area, near where Lewisburg Pike crosses the train tracks, and fanning southward, saw some of the bloodiest fighting of the battle.

After the McNutt house burned to the ground in 1865, William O'Neal Perkins, one of the wealthy Williamson County Perkinses, purchased the land to build a large and imposing Italianate residence for himself and his wife.

Timing is everything in life, and William O'Neal Perkins's timing could simply not have been worse. He thought life would get back to "normal" in the South in the years following the Civil War, but there was a "new normal" for the formerly wealthy land- and slave-owners of the antebellum South. Money was scarce, and very soon Mr. Perkins could not afford to keep the house. So he downsized, swapping houses with an up-and-comer named William Winstead, who called his grand new abode Winstead Manor. The house later changed hands several more times.

Eloise Pitts O'More's beloved Abbey Leix Mansion is the centerpiece of the college that bears her name.

The last person who lived in the house was Eloise Pitts O'More, who founded O'More College and operated it out of the house—and some say, is still there. Mrs. O'More was a Fayetteville, Tennessee, native who traveled to Paris in 1924 at the age of 18 to study art and architecture. She returned to the U.S. and much later, in 1970, founded O'More College. In 1979 she moved the school to Winstead Manor, which she renamed Abbey Leix after her husband's ancestral home in Ireland.

Mrs. O'More retired in 1994 but remained involved in the school's operations. She continued to live upstairs in the house until she could no longer climb stairs. The school then built her a first floor suite of rooms—bedroom, kitchen and bathroom—so she could continue to live in her house. Mrs. O'More died in 2002 at the age of 95.

Sandra Kiger's first day on the job as O'More's dean of business affairs was a bit portentous. She arrived at 7:00 a.m., ahead of the rest of the staff, let herself in and waited for a staff person to show her around and get her situated. She heard someone typing upstairs—really typing, on an old-fashioned manual typewriter—not a computer keyboard. When the other person arrived Sandra mentioned what she heard and just got a funny look in return: not only had no one else been there, but they also didn't have any old-fashioned typewriters.

Sandra's office was in Mrs. O'More's old bedroom; tiny Mrs. O'More slept in a little alcove next to Sandra's desk. Sandra does not particularly believe in ghosts, and was not afraid or alarmed, but she said, pointing to the alcove, "She's here."

When Sandra returned to school after a vacation or school break and unlocked the door to her office for the first time, she was often assailed by a peculiar odor. A former facilities manager, Tom Stein, checked the crawl space and found nothing that would produce such a smell. To Sandra, it was the smell of death. Once they came in after Christmas break and found an unexplainable brown substance oozing down the wall. It all happens in Mrs. O'More's former bedroom.

Lauren Rauter, today owner of the hip Main Street stationary and paper shop Rock Paper Scissors, was chair of the fashion department at O'More from 1998-2002.

Someone likes to have O'More's Library to himself after hours.

"It was either the fall of '99 or spring of 2000 when I was working late in my office on the second floor of the library one evening," Lauren remembers. "I thought I was alone but I kept hearing footsteps on the stairs."

Was a student locked in? Was there someone else there Lauren didn't know about? So she went downstairs to check.

Lauren found no one, and after checking to make sure the front door was locked, she went back upstairs to her office. Then she heard it again, a creaking noise on the stairs, much like the sound she heard during the day as people walked up and down the stairs.

Suddenly, a voice in her office commanded: *Get out!* The voice was muffled, like a loud whisper, but distinct.

"I was like, 'Huh? What?' I don't know who, or how, but I wasn't staying. I got out."

Lauren grabbed her keys, ran out of the building and raced home. In her haste that night, she left her purse and laptop behind. She never stayed late again.

Almost a decade later, Lauren remains positive she heard someone commanding her to leave the building…and there was no one there.

I related that story on a ghost tour in September, 2010. We usually don't go to O'More on tours, but because Franklin's annual Jazz Festival Labor Day weekend makes touring Third Avenue next to impossible, we headed down Second and ended up on the college's campus.

Afterwards, a woman said to me, "Something happened there." That's all—*something happened there*. I asked her to elaborate, but she refused. I could tell she had more to say, but she clammed up. It struck me as a bit odd, but I quickly forgot about it.

Monday morning she called me from Michigan. She said, "I want to tell you what I *wanted* to tell you on Saturday. I kept hearing the name George . . . he's feeling a little misunderstood. He was concerned about her, because of what happened there before in the battle that took place there. He's stuck in the past. He was upset with her because she was afraid of him. He wasn't trying to frighten her. He was protective of her."

Aha! That's why he told her to leave: the fighting had started and she was in danger— *in his reality*.

Tom Stein most emphatically does not believe in ghosts. But he can't explain what happened late one night when he was in the library. He lived on campus and his personal computer was acting "weird." The student computers are on the same network and he thought he would check and see if they were also acting up.

It was 1 a.m. when he unlocked a side door to the building and went inside. He sat down to check of the computers when two things happened simultaneously.

"All six of the student computers turned on," he said. "They all bypassed the password, went past the home page and opened on Yahoo."

At the same time, Tom heard footsteps on the other side of a wall. "The footsteps were deliberately loud—like someone stomping—is all I can say."

Tom went around the wall and "someone was there. Not physically there, but someone was there. The hair stood up on the back of my neck. I went right home and had a beer."

Tom cannot explain how it all happened. It made him feel very uncomfortable.

"I'm a Christian and this doesn't make sense. I don't think anything's going to harm me but I just don't like it. I won't go in that building at night. For all of the computers to turn on at once was weird. There was energy or something in the house. The doors were all locked except the one I opened and I was sitting right next to it. No one had been in the building for hours and the computers only stay up for 10 minutes. The screens weren't on when I walked in and I didn't touch them.

"I don't believe in this stuff . . . but this is unexplainable."

So . . . it seems as if Mrs. O'More is definitely in the office, her former bedroom. But the library? That just doesn't sound like the petite Mrs. O'More, with the big stomping footfall and urgent command. Indeed, it sounds like a soldier, marching, like so many marched in Franklin during the Civil War.

Chapter 9

Bloody Franklin

S ometimes ghosts and spirits arise from tragedy, from lives cut short and unfinished business. In that sense it's difficult to imagine a place more likely to give rise to ghosts and haunts than a battlefield. Young men, their lives in front of them, are called to sacrifice themselves to a greater cause. These were young men who like all young men had dreams and hopes and plans, the wife or sweetheart back home, perhaps. Many of these dreams died on the battlefield of Franklin.

November 30, 1864's Battle of Franklin was described by *National Geographic* Magazine in 2005 as the "most unjustly forgotten battle of the entire Civil War." Indeed, even some Franklin residents today don't realize the significance of the abbreviated, desperate and bloody battle that ended the daring plan of Confederate General John Bell Hood to retake Nashville from the Union.

Make no mistake: Those who lived through it never forgot it as long as they lived.

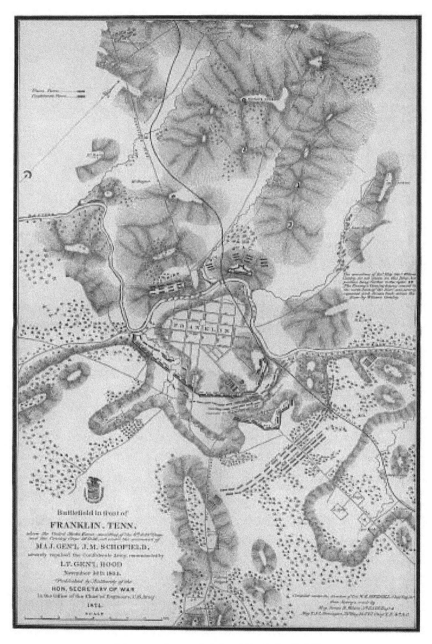

Union General John M. Schofield's
map of the battlefield of Franklin

Alice McPhail Nichol cowered, terrified, in the basement of the Carter House during the battle. She said, many years later, "You know how little eight-year-old girls don't remember much after 65 years have passed by, but there are some things that impress a child and they never forget it and that one thing is the Battle of Franklin."

One soldier proclaimed that "it was as if the devil had full possession of the earth." A child said, "It was so loud you couldn't hear yourself scream."

Tennessee's capital city fell to the Union army in February 1862. The Union army built four forts in Nashville and directed the western theater of the war from it. Nashville became the "Supply Depot of the West" as the city's Second Avenue warehouses bulged with food, medicine, supplies, arms and ammunition,

The Confederacy needed Nashville back—as well as the supplies and war matériel held there—and Confederate President Jefferson Davis decided that John Bell Hood was the man to do it. Hood had lost Atlanta in July, 1864, and hoped retaking Nashville would redeem both the Confederate cause as well as his own reputation. The end game for "Hood's Tennessee Campaign" was to move into Kentucky, then Ohio, and then head over the mountains to help Lee, currently struggling in Virginia.

That's what brought two armies—20,000 Confederate and 22,000 Union soldiers—together in Franklin. It was a race to Nashville. Why Franklin? Simply put: it was an accident of geography culminating in a perfect storm.

Generals John Schofield and John Bell Hood were classmates at West Point; Schofield even tutored Hood for a time.

After the Atlanta debacle, Hood's army headed north from Alabama in late November, 1864.

Union General John M. Schofield also raced toward Nashville from Atlanta. On November 28, he held Columbia, Tennessee, 50 miles south of Nashville. Hood evaded the Federals there and arrived in Spring Hill, cutting the distance between his army and Nashville by a third.

The army bivouacked in Spring Hill and a satisfied Hood went to bed in a friendly plantation home secure in the knowledge that two more days of marching would find his men on the threshold of Nashville.

John Bell Hood lost a leg at Chickamauga and the use of an arm at Gettysburg. He was back in the saddle just six weeks after the amputation of his leg; every morning his men strapped him to his horse. After the war he married and had 11 children in 10 years before dying in New Orleans of yellow fever along with his wife and oldest daughter.

Schofield's army arrived in Spring Hill on the heels of Hood's army. The night was as dark as the inside of a cave. Schofield told his weary men to keep marching. They did. They marched through the night, past Hood's army sleeping mere yards from the road they traversed, all 22,000 men, 700 wagons, cannons, artillery, horses, mules . . . and no one stopped them. The Federal force, marching up Columbia Pike, arrived in Franklin the morning of November 30.

The serene and tranquil Carter House today belies the horrors of November 30, 1864. Today a historic house museum, the State of Tennessee bought the house when it was to be torn down for a gas station.

Geography was Destiny

Schofield surveyed the landscape from the yard of a man named Fountain Branch Carter, owner of a 300-acre farm one-half mile from Franklin's downtown. Carter's 1830 Greek Revival-style farmhouse is situated at the top of a gentle rise south of Franklin that then drops down southward and continues away from town, then rises up again to meet Winstead Hill. Schofield never intended to stop in Franklin, but he discovered that the only two bridges crossing the Harpeth River were severely damaged, and the river at flood level, trapping his army with its back to the river. He set about getting the bridge to Nashville repaired, and ordered his weary men to build a wall of breastworks just south of the Carter Farm.

That same morning, Hood awoke to the news that the Union army had slipped by his sleeping army. From all accounts, he was livid, "wrathy as a rattlesnake." He excoriated his subordinates and accused the men of cowardice. He ordered double-time marching north to Nashville.

When Hood arrived at Franklin he galloped his horse up Winstead Hill, pulled out his spyglass and scanned the fields to the north. What the commander saw had to give him pause. His army was facing two miles of cleared farm fields. It was mid-afternoon three weeks from the winter solstice; light would soon fade. He knew the Union army had greater numbers and better weapons, including the impressive Spencer repeating rifle. He could see well-fortified breastworks that would protect the Northern soldiers as they fired on the charging Confederates. Hood rode back down the hill and met with his

Tod Carter had a cocky side. He wrote a letter to a cousin: "Tell Miss Fanny Park not to accept Phil because when I get home she will surely have a chance at me!"

division commanders at the Harrison House, an early 19th century plantation house just south of Winstead Hill. Meeting in the front right parlor and ignoring vigorous and vociferous objections from his staff, Hood made the decision to attack.

The charge began in the late afternoon, as the Confederate army, flags waving, bands playing and shrieking the Rebel yell, marched to the front in a full frontal assault.

Among the men was a 24-year-old army captain named Theodrick Carter, one of three sons of Fountain Branch. "Tod" was a fiery secessionist and talented young lawyer who wrote a pro-secessionist column for a Chattanooga newspaper under the pen name Mint Julep. As he led his men into battle, Tod Carter cried, "Follow me boys, I'm almost home!"

Generals John Adams, Patrick Cleburne, Otho Strahl, John Carter, States Rights Gist and Hiram Granbury likewise led their men into the battle and perished in it.

General Patrick Cleburne lost favor with the Confederate high command when he proposed arming slaves to fight for the South in exchange for their freedom.

One of the most beloved by his men of all officers, Patrick Cleburne said to his brigade commander Daniel Govan, "Well, Govan, if we are to die, let us die like men."

In town all was chaos. Union sympathizer Fannie Courtney lived on South Margin Street one block off Columbia Pike. She reported to the Union command in Nashville four months later:

"About half past three o'clock I was sitting at my dinner table, when I heard the roar of artillery. I ran to the yard to listen. There was skirmishing for a few minutes only, when, with a tremendous yell, the rebels made a charge upon the whole line. The bullets were falling so thick it was unsafe to remain longer. I stood within the door, and in a few minutes all was in perfect confusion. Men, women and children were running in every direction with unmanageable teams, loose horses and mules."

The Courtneys and their neighbors hastened to the protection of the cellar.

Top to bottom, Generals Otho Strahl, States Right Gist and Hiram Granbury, three of the six generals killed at Franklin, the most of any battle in the entire war.

Fannie Courtney later married U.S. Lt. Col. George Grummond, Franklin's provost marshal during the war. But it didn't end well. The next year he was killed fighting Indians in Wyoming. Upon applying for a widow's pension she discovered he was already married.

"Later, I went to the door, and within a few yards of me lay a Federal soldier. I sent one of the soldiers out to look after his comrade and to give him water. But he did not have to remain long; the wound proved to be fatal, and the poor man soon expired. Another desperate charge! Such yells! I can never forget them," Fannie said.

The battle lasted just five hours. It ended when the Union army completed the bridge repairs and withdrew as ordered, marching through the night to Nashville. Hood was jubilant, thinking his audacious plan had worked. He wired Jefferson Davis news of the victory. But the numbers told the tale: of the nearly 10,000 men killed, wounded, captured or missing, almost 8,000 were Confederates. Six generals were killed, the most of any battle in the war. The command structure was in shambles. The Confederate Army of Tennessee, as an effective fighting force, was no more.

The war in the West was over.

The Aftermath

The task of burying the dead and tending to the wounded fell to what remained of the Army of Tennessee and caring townspeople.

Fannie Courtney remembered:

"Early the next morning after the Battle I went to the field. The sight was dreadful. It seemed I could scarcely move for fear of stepping on men either dead or wounded. Some were cold and stiff, others with the lifeblood ebbing out, unconscious of all around, while others were writhing in agony, calling 'Water! Water!' I can hear them even now."

Franklin teenager Hardin Figuers said, "Men, shot and wounded in every part of the body, were crying out for help, telling their names and calling for friends to help them. It was a weird and gruesome sight."

A soldier said, "The dead, cold and stiff bodies were laying in every conceivable posture, all with ghastly faces and glassy eyes. Some [were] in a sitting attitude, braced with the dead bodies of their comrades. Streets, gutters, sideway, doorstones and porticoes [were] covered with dead men in blue."

Moscow Carter, Tod's brother, said, "In trying to clear up, I scraped together a half bushel of brains right around the house and the whole place was dyed with blood."

John Adams was found astride his horse straddling the breastworks, man and beast both dead. Tod Carter's father and uncle found their son and nephew on the battlefield, life ebbing out of him, and carried him to the bed he was born in, where he died surrounded by his family.

Outside on the cold hard ground, men died alone and far from home.

Confederate General Frank Cheatham said, "The dead were stacked like wheat and scattered like sheathes of grain. You could walk on the field on the bodies without touching the ground. I never saw a field like that, and I never want to see a field like that again."

Today the Franklin battlefield is largely developed, with subdivisions and shopping centers and every manner of commerce. Most of the historic downtown, plus everything south to Winstead Hill and the Harrison House and spreading out two miles wide at the bottom, is core battlefield.

Is it any wonder Franklin is Tennessee's most haunted town?

There are hundreds of bullet holes on this and other Carter buildings, making these buildings the most bullet-riddled of any structures in the United States.

OLD SMOKE HOUSE, SCENE OF THE BATTLE OF FRANKLIN,
NOTE THE BULLET HOLES IN THE WALLS, FRANKLIN, TENN.

Written on this old postcard of the Carter House smoke house: "Note the bullet holes in the walls."

Sheltering Houses, Sheltering Spirits

The Harrison House, the private dwelling where Hood announced his decision to fight at Franklin, is today the home of Pam Lewis. Owner of the house since 1993, Pam is convinced there are several spirits inhabiting the building.

The first indication came during renovations, when the floors were being refurbished.

"The floor refinisher was the only person in the house when he saw a reflection of a bearded man in a mirror. He refused to finish the job," said Pam. A mist has appeared over a bed in a "secret" room in the house discovered years later during renovations. Pam believes a female spy ring operated from this room.

In the right front room where Hood planned the battle, Pam and her family and friends have heard voices and footsteps and felt cold areas. Wall art and paintings have been found askew or crooked and leaning against the floor. Silk flowers were tossed onto the floor from vases. Lights flicker unexplainably and bulbs are loosened in their sockets.

Generals argued before the battle and one died
afterward at the Harrison House. Sometimes it seems
they're still around.

"More activity seems to happen in November and December," Pam reports. The battle was fought November 30, of course, and Harrison House, like so many, was used as a hospital. In fact, General John C. Carter (no relation to the Franklin Carter family), was mortally wounded in the Battle of Franklin and taken to Harrison House where he died December 10 in an upstairs bedroom.

In the room where Carter convalesced and died a television set randomly turned itself on. It happened so often that Pam felt compelled to remove it. Water turned itself on in the sink and ran and ran. Pam and others also have seen apparitions of soldiers in upstairs bedrooms and have heard footsteps up and down the front steps. Once a VCR flew off a shelf.

But not every sighting seems to involve the battle. Pam once saw what appeared to be the spirits of an elderly couple sitting on the sofa and the apparition of a woman sitting at the piano. Pam was once visited by a psychic who asked the woman her name.

"Madeleine," the woman replied.

"When did you live here?" the psychic asked.

"I *didn't* live here. I *live* here."

Pam checked the records, and a woman named Madeleine did once live in the house. Pam notes that the spirits have calmed since she had the house blessed.

The Carter House, near the epicenter of the Battle of Franklin, is today a historic house museum. It has also had many reports of spectral sightings. Some of the sightings are of young children, particularly a mischievous little girl, and also women, which do not seem to relate to the battle. A decorative painter involved in the restoration of the house heard her name called by a woman's voice several times as she worked alone in the house. However, several visitors over the years have reported seeing the spirit of a young man, swathed in bandages, lying in or sitting on the edge of Tod Carter's deathbed.

Lotz House Spirits Linger

The Lotz House is located just north of the Carter House on the east side of Columbia Pike. Completed in 1858, the house was built as a "show house" by master carpenter and piano maker Johann Albert Lotz, a German immigrant. Every mantel is different; the newel post on the staircase is a piano leg. Potential customers came to Lotz's house and chose their designs by viewing and examining the woodwork in his house.

On the morning of the battle, a Union officer knocked on the front door and "offered to do some yard work," as J.T. Thompson, current owner of the house, wryly relates. The soldiers leveled the Lotzes' detached kitchen, outhouse, sheds, barn, and woodworking shop, and took all that wood as well as his inventory of fine poplar, cherry and oak. The soldiers threw all of the wood into the breastworks for fortification.

Johann Lotz decided that because his house was planked, it would probably not survive cannonading. So he, his wife and three children ran across the road to their friends the Carters, whose house was even closer to the line of battle but made of sturdier brick. The Lotzes holed up there, spending a terrifying night in the basement with the Carter family, servants and friends.

The Lotz house did survive, but not unscathed. At least two cannon balls came through the roof. Both passed through the second floor and came to rest on the first floor, burning their images into the wood. Still visible on the second floor are two patches, one 4' x 4' and the other a bit smaller.

The staircase in the center hall fell to the first floor. Bloodstains mar the floors throughout the house, including one of a person in the fetal position. The entire south wall, facing the withering fire of the attacking Confederates, was destroyed. When the Lotz family came back to their house the next

morning, it was open to the elements from the roof, one whole side was gone, and the staircase was unusable.

The wood patch on the second floor was clearly not Johann Lotz's best work.

This six pound cannon ball sits next to the deep scar made on the ground floor of the Lotz House.

Johann Lotz hastily repaired the damage as well as he could, but the work does not reach the level of craftsmanship he exhibited in the past. He just did the best he could, under the circumstances.

Johann and his family stayed in Franklin four years after the war ended, as he struggled to rebuild his home and business. Then, in 1869, he was asked to make a piano. He carved the piano with an eagle, wings and talons outstretched, and flanked on both sides by flags, on one side Old Glory, the other the Stars and Bars. It appeared that one of the eagle's talons was grasping the Confederate flag, as if indicating domination (although it was probably only the wood grain making it appear that way). At any rate, upon completion, word got out that Johann Lotz had made a piano that disrespected the Confederacy.

Members of the local Ku Klux Klan paid him a visit. The Klan decided to make an example of Johann Lotz and threatened to tar and feather him in his front yard. Within days, Johann sold everything he owned, including the house, packed up his family in a covered wagon and escaped to San Jose, California 2,300 miles away.

J.T. Thompson, his wife Susan Andrews Thompson and his mother Sue Thompson purchased the house in 2002 to save it from becoming a restaurant called "Lotz of Tacos," and planning eventually to open it as a house museum.

"We'd owned it less than a month; it was in 2002. I wanted to spend the night in the house on the anniversary of the battle," J.T. recalled.

J.T., Susan, his mother Sue and daughter Shelby and Susan's sister Peggy were all there on November 30, along with blow-up mattresses on which to sleep. It was early evening, about 7 p.m.

Nobody knows who Ann is, but someone was still looking
for her at the Lotz House on November 30, 2002.

"Peggy and I were standing in the entryway. We heard drums, duh dut duh duh, dutdutdutdut duh," J.T. said. "We thought it was the reenactors marching from Winstead Hill to the Carter House like they do every year."

But it was 7 p.m. and the march had concluded several hours before.

"Then we thought it had to be something from the Carter House, but we went outside and there were no drums. That was the first odd thing."

Susan picked up the story here. "We heard it again and went back outside. There was still no drum sound outside. Then we realized the sound was from upstairs; it could only be heard from inside. We were all thinking, 'Isn't that strange?'

"We weren't there to see if the house was haunted," Susan said, who adds that she was skeptical on the subject of ghosts before her experiences that night.

However, Shelby had come prepared; she brought a Ouija board.

"Shelby started asking questions. She was just pushing the thing around, so Susan and I tried it. I asked it to describe what happened here," J.T. recalled.

"V-I. These letters spelled out and we stopped. Susan and I looked at each other. We asked each other, 'Are you doing this?' Neither one of us was. So we kept at it. L-E were the next two letters. That was all. Vile. That's not a word people use much anymore. We don't.

"Then we asked it how many people died. M-A-N-Y. Many. And that was it."

After everyone had gone to sleep in a downstairs bedroom (except Peggy who had departed), something—she doesn't know what—woke up Susan in the middle of the night. From where she had been sleeping, she could see the staircase in the center hall. On the landing was an ethereal form.

"There was a ghostly figure of a woman in a grungy white sleeping gown, holding a candle in a holder. She was looking straight ahead, calling out, 'Where's Ann, where's Ann?'"

Susan woke up J.T. but by the time he was able to look, the figure had disappeared.

"There's no doubt in my mind what it was. It wasn't scary, just creepy. I think there's something to restless souls," Susan said.

"I absolutely do believe now. I had it happen to me. I don't care if other people don't believe me. But it did happen."

For the first six years the Thompsons owned the Lotz House, they rented it to a firm of lawyers. When the museum opened in October, 2008, J.T. and his mother Sue began operating the site. Early on, J.T. learned to "give them an audience on the front end and back end," meaning saying hello in the morning and goodbye in the evening to the spirits that they believe inhabit the house.

One morning J. T. was running late for an appointment with a computer tech. Carrying a cup of coffee, J. T. hurried inside and took the tech upstairs to his computer. He returned downstairs and then came back up about 15 minutes later because he realized he'd left his coffee on the desk upstairs. The tech's face was ashen; his eyes were staring. J.T. asked, "Can I call a doctor? You look ill." The man said, "Your coffee cup just moved a foot in front of me!"

"There's a simple explanation for this," J.T. explained. "I was in such a hurry I forgot to greet them when I came in this morning."

J.T. Thompson, above, knows just how to deal with the ghosts in his building: he always acknowledges their presence.

In the process of opening the museum in the fall of 2008, J.T. often brought tools, including screwdrivers, to work on the building. He'd bring one, lose it, bring another, lose it, until finally he had brought a grand total of 5 screwdrivers to the Lotz House, and couldn't find a single one. Several days after the last one disappeared, they reappeared on a window sill, all lined up in a row.

His checkbook went missing. He searched the building, his car, his home, it was gone. Two weeks later, he came in as usual one morning and there was the checkbook, "right smack dab" in the middle of his desk.

Experiences Not Always Welcome

A woman picked up this book at the Main Street Festival in April, 2008 where it was first sold after publication.

"Ghosts in Franklin?" she asked. "Are there ghosts in Franklin?" I said, yes, many folks have had these experiences. Then she told me hers.

She had been living in a bungalow on one of the streets off Columbia Avenue several months when it all started. She would stir in the night because it felt like someone or something was gently touching her neck and check. At first she thought it was a dream until one night she opened her eyes. There in the corner of her room was the ghost of a Confederate soldier.

"Not a whole ghost, part of one. It was his body from the knees up and he was missing part of his neck. I was terrified."

The woman screamed, said the Lord's Prayer over and over and he vanished. But he always returned, every few weeks or months as she awoke to a soft touch on her neck.

After awhile it wasn't so much scary as sad, as she could sense his feelings of sorrow and loss. Then she noticed that he wasn't looking at her; he seemed to be looking for someone or something off in the distance. Finally, it occurred to her what the matter was, and she decided that the next time he appeared to her, she was going to talk to him.

The occasion presented itself several weeks later when he made his presence known.

"I get the feeling you're looking for someone you know," she said to the ghost. "Whoever it is, is dead and has gone to heaven. It's time for you to quit looking for him and go to heaven too. Everyone you knew has died and gone to heaven and they are all waiting for you. So it's time to go now. Go!"

He seemed for a few seconds to be taking it all in. Then he disappeared. She lived in the house for two more years and he never came back. The man just didn't know he was dead.

Fred was six years old and standing on the back porch of his house on Fairgrounds Street off Columbia Avenue five decades ago at dusk one summer evening. Off in the distance appeared a misty figure riding a horse.

"It was a soldier who was wearing an old-looking uniform, with a feather on his hat. I could see a sword hanging off his belt," Fred remembers. He watched the man for 30-45 seconds before the horse and rider finally disappeared into the twilight.

This 1890s Kurz and Allison print of the Battle of Franklin doesn't quite get the topography right but the fighting is gruesomely accurate.

"He didn't look real," Fred said, then added. "I really don't believe in ghosts, but I know I saw one!"

And it certainly wasn't a welcome experience. "To this day I've never seen anything else like it," Fred shuddered as he spoke. "And I don't want to."

A local real estate agent who once lived in a 1930s house on Jennings Street asked me if I knew anything about the house's history. He said he would hear strange, unexpected sounds such as thuds and bangs and rattling at the windows. He said the sounds were unlike anything one would expect even in an older house. It was as if "someone" was trying to get inside but nobody you could call 911 for. At the time I said I didn't know of anything having happened in the house that would lead to such manifestations but later it hit me: this house sits at ground zero on the battlefield.

A woman who lived in a house on Battle Avenue, between Columbia Avenue and West Main Street, reported sensing a presence in her house, and sometimes seeing the image of a person in a mirror. She said she would just catch it out of the corner of her eye, but it was definitely a person's reflection. *Battle* Avenue? Guess how it got its name?

The basement of a commercial building on Columbia Avenue just south of Lotz House proved frightful for a young man who adventurously planned to spend the night there after hearing stories about it being haunted. He bailed out after several hours of frightening occurrences including yelling and screaming, and ran outside to find his windshield wipers swinging and headlights blinking.

These ghostly experiences were certainly startling and often frightening to those who experienced them. Most would agree that whatever fear they felt paled in comparison to the terror forever seared into the memories of those who lived through the Battle of Franklin—and some who didn't.

Chapter 9

She Watches Still

C arnton Plantation was the largest of 44 Franklin homes, churches, stores and offices that were eventually used as field hospitals for the wounded.

Carnton was built in 1826 by Randal McGavock, a member of a prominent founding family of Tennessee. Randal named his federal-style dwelling Carnton after the family's ancestral home in Ireland.

The dictionary defines "cairn," the root word of Carnton, as a heap of stones set up as a landmark, monument or tombstone. When he named it in 1826, Randal McGavock could not have imagined that 40 years later that's exactly what Carnton would become.

About noon on the day of the Battle of Franklin, Loring's Division of the Army of Tennessee peeled off from the main body of the Army at Henpeck Lane, about three miles south of Franklin. They headed east on Henpeck, then wheeled north on Lewisburg Pike, and began to cross the southern fields of Carnton.

Carrie Winder was 19 and engaged to be married to John McGavock when her portrait was painted by Nashville painter Washington Cooper. Oddly, she insisted on wearing black, the color of mourning, for her engagement portrait.

Randal's son and heir John now owned Carnton. He lived at the house with his wife Carrie and their two young children, Hattie and Winder. Today Carnton is within the city limits of Franklin, but in 1864, it was "out in the country." On this day, it was impossible to learn about the situation in town, and naturally the family was anxious. They worried about their children. They also had a governess in the house as well as a young cousin who had been sent out from Nashville by her parents for safekeeping. Everyone knew a big battle was coming, but Nashville was the object. No one expected Franklin.

So Carrie, desperate for information, posted herself at her front gate, and watched as the soldiers passed around her house, with Carnton like an island in the stream of soldiers passing right and left. Suddenly, Carrie heard the loud crack of a weapon firing at what seemed like close proximity. Alarmed, she ran for safety on the porch. A Confederate officer rode into the yard in an effort to reassure her that neither she nor the house was being fired upon. When he dismounted, and they looked at each other, to their utter surprise they turned out to be old friends from Louisiana. His name was Col. Thomas Markham and he was not optimistic about the chances for success in the looming battle. He told Carrie that the order would soon be given to attack, and that there would be an immediate need for a field hospital behind the line. Carrie volunteered Carnton. Markham wrote later:

"This recognition, so welcome and so grateful in that strait, led to this selection of our division field hospital and secured for our suffering men the shelter and care of a noble home and ministering attentions of as princely a man and queenly a woman as [I've ever known]. All that was theirs in that great house was ours . . . They opened their hearts and their home."

The wounded were brought to Carnton within an hour of the first shot. By midnight the house was overflowing with wounded and dying soldiers, 300 at any given time. Reserving one room for her family, Carrie devoted herself to the wounded, moving among the men, offering food, coffee, tea, prayers and words of comfort. She gathered her fine linens, underclothing and husband's shirts for use as bandages for the doctors.

Throughout the house surgeons operated, amputating arms and legs. Oral tradition relates that surgeons tossed the severed limbs out of the second floor window. After 48 hours the pile reached the height of the second floor window sill.

The bodies of four Confederate generals—Patrick Cleburne, Otho Strahl, John Adams and Hiram Granbury—were brought to Carnton and laid out on the back porch for their men to pay their respects.

"During all this time, the surgeons plied their dreadful work," wrote Confederate Colonel W. D. Gale about Carrie in a letter to his wife, "…yet amid it all, this noble woman, the very impersonation of divine sympathy and tender pity, was active and constantly at work….During the night neither she nor any of her household slept…. Unaffrighted by the sight of blood, unawed by horrid wounds, unblanched by ghastly death, she walked from room to room, from man to man, her very skirts stained with blood, the incarnation of pity and mercy. Is it strange that all who were there call her blessed?"

Wounded soldiers remained at Carnton days, weeks and even months. Life had changed forever.

Everywhere, it was death and dying. The short but bloody Battle of Franklin and its aftermath were forever burned into the minds of those who witnessed it. Recovery was a long time coming to Franklin.

Today Carrie McGavock lives on as *The Widow of the South* (2005). Written by preservationist and long-time Carnton supporter Robert Hicks, the book is a historical novel based on the Battle of Franklin, Carrie McGavock and Carnton and their role during the battle and its aftermath, including the creation of the Confederate cemetery.

Carnton remained in the McGavock family until 1911. After it was sold, the McGavocks moved to a house in downtown Franklin, leaving their almost century-old home and its memories behind.

THE McGAVOCK RESIDENCE, FRANKLIN, TENN.

Carnton, photographed here about 1907, sheltered hundreds of wounded soldiers after the Battle of Franklin.

Throughout much of the 20th century Carnton was absentee-owned. The last private owner of the house was a retired doctor who lived in Florida; he always intended to restore the house but never got around to it. The house was in terrible shape by the late 1970s and the land around it was threatened by development.

Finally, a small but committed group of local preservationists convinced the owner to donate the house to an association they established to save the house. The house has been fully restored and furnished with much original and period furniture, wallpaper, fabrics, paint and decorative and personal objects. Carnton is now a historic house museum where visitors learn the story of Carnton and the McGavocks' role after the Battle of Franklin.

Visitors to the house and its 48 acres have reported strange experiences and ghostly sightings since it was opened to the public. Many of these stories are well-known in the annals of ghost stories in Tennessee, leading some people to claim that Carnton is the most haunted building in Tennessee. While working at Carnton I was contacted by many people with ghost stories. The first three years I worked at Carnton I conducted occasional ghost tours in addition to my regular duties. Visitors would relate odd experiences before, during and after their tours. These were stories I did not have to search out; they came to me.

The Guardian of the Cemetery

In January, 2005 my then-business partner René and I led our very first ghost tour at the plantation. In period dress, we directed very enthusiastic groups of ghost hunters through the house and cemetery. My daughter Anne was home from college for the weekend and had accompanied us to Carnton to run the visitor center.

It was about 10:30 p.m. and Anne was ready to go home. She walked out on the porch of the visitor center, which is about 50 yards directly behind the back porch of the historic house, and scanned the landscape in the darkness looking for us in the cemetery. The cemetery is farther behind the visitor center and about 200 yards to the west.

"I heard someone walking," she said. "I thought it was you coming back from the cemetery."

But it wasn't; she looked around the corner at the cemetery and saw only the flickers of flashlights and flash photography among the gravestones.

"Then I realized the sound was coming from the house."

She turned back to face the house, and there she saw a figure "shuffling" across the second floor balcony.

"It was a woman, not young, not old. She was wearing a pink, long-sleeved gown, like a nightgown," Anne told us. "My first thought was it was you or René, but I knew we had already locked and alarmed the house and you were in the cemetery and René had already left . . . and I knew I was seeing a ghost."

Anne's feet turned to lead. She could not move. Then the motion light on the visitor center porch turned off, leaving her in blackness. At that, her adrenalin kicked in and she raced to the cemetery to find us, where she breathlessly related her experience (The ghost hunters thought it was quite unfair that they hadn't been present for this appearance. Anne thought it unfair that she had been).

Later, I asked Anne, "Did she look at you? Do you think she saw you?"

"Oh, no, not at all," Anne remembers. "She wasn't looking at me at all. She just looked off in the direction of the cemetery, and then she smiled and waved."

Carrie McGavock? Still keeping watch over the cemetery? Anne thinks so, and she's not the only one.

One day nearly 20 years ago, a volunteer we'll call Janet was the last person at Carnton at the end of the day. At the time the visitor center was not in a separate building. The present dining room had not yet been restored and it was used for staff offices and visitor center. At closing time she was downstairs ready to leave the house when she heard someone walking around upstairs.

Janet walked upstairs and checked the four bedrooms; they were empty.

"Then I felt drawn to the sitting room upstairs," Janet recalled. The room she referred to is at the front of the house opposite the staircase. It is believed to have been used as a sitting or possibly a dressing room. There is a jib window that opens onto a porch over the front door of the house.

Janet walked into the room, looked around, and found nothing out of order. Puzzled, she went downstairs and left the house by the front, rather than the usual back door. Janet walked down the brick walk toward the front gate when she suddenly turned around and looked back at the house.

There, peering out the window in the second floor sitting room was a woman dressed in white. She was holding back a curtain with her hand, her head tilted to the side. For just a second the two women's eyes met, then the woman let go of the curtain and Janet didn't see her again. She believes it was Carrie McGavock.

A delivery man once asked me if anyone had ever seen a ghost at Carnton.

"Oh yes," I said, "We hear that a lot. Why do you ask?"

George had been with the sheriff's department in the early 1980s. At the time Carnton was outside Franklin's city limits and under the jurisdiction of the county.

"We used to patrol every night just to make sure no one was messing around at Carnton," George said. "In the two years I was a deputy I saw a female spirit up there on the balcony three separate times," he said, pointing at the second floor porch on the left.

"Outside the master bedroom?" I asked.

"I didn't know that's what it was but yes, there," he said. "I always thought it had to be the woman of the house. She seemed protective somehow."

She Followed Him Home

Carrie McGavock influenced many during her life. One contemporary described her as an angel of mercy, the Good Samaritan of Williamson County. Over 120 years later, she transformed a modern college student.

In 1988 a young man we'll call Rick and his father visited Rick's brother, a Vanderbilt medical resident, in Nashville. At the suggestion of his sister-in-law, they visited Carnton.

The portrait of Carrie McGavock, described as "mesmerizing" by some visitors, is the focal point of the family parlor, which also includes the McGavock family Bible, in which are recorded births, marriages and deaths from the early 19ᵗʰ century to the late 20ᵗʰ century.

As they began their tour Rick had a shocking realization: a spirit was present, accompanying him throughout the house.

It was "very alarming for me. Alarming in that it really shook up my world view of things and in particular the hereafter. I had no explanation of it," Rick said.

Rick felt not only the spirit's existence but also its emotion as it followed him; he remembers "knowing" that this person felt grief in some fashion and could also tell it was a feminine spirit. Then he saw the portrait of Carrie McGavock on the wall and knew that's who it was.

She remained with them as they drove away. Rick had a vision of the spirit hovering over his dad's car, and adds: "I have never had that happen as you can guess."

In the middle of the night, as he lay sleeping on his brother's sofa, Rick awoke to find she was standing right next to him.

Rick told her he was sorry for all the pain she had suffered in her life. After that, she "shot through" his body, and he says, "for the first time I realized I had a soul."

Carrie then spoke his name. "When she said it she conveyed emotion to me such that I felt her inside. I felt sorrow but also appreciation, I felt goodness and a very nice feeling that she was a very nice spirit."

Rick felt "paralyzed" for awhile, then eventually went back to sleep, and in the morning she was gone.

Looking back, Rick knows "it was a very highly intense personal experience that I will never forget. It was not scary either. Indeed I look upon it with fondness and wonder."

The Weeping Maiden

Fondness and wonder are perhaps not the words Shelly Robertson uses to describe one curious day at Carnton as a youngster.

Shelly Robertson and her friend Maddie were 12 years old when they volunteered at Carnton during summer vacation.

The girls were not old enough to conduct tours so Bernice Seiberling, Carnton's director, usually put them to work dusting furniture. Typically at the end of the day she asked them to make a run-through of the house, checking to make sure everyone was out of the building.

It was a normal day. At closing time Shelly and Maddie walked upstairs together; Maddie went into the guest room on the right side; Shelly to the master bedroom on the left. She then turned toward a connecting door leading to the nursery, which has access from both the master bedroom and hallway.

As Shelly turned, she saw the figure of a woman in the room.

"She was standing in front of the window, facing out. She had on an old-fashioned brown dress with a hoop skirt," Shelly recalls. "I didn't know what to think."

She ran out to get Maddie and brought her back. Maddie saw her too. The two girls then raced downstairs to tell the director what they'd seen.

"You've just seen the Weeping Maiden," Mrs. Seiberling told them. "You're not the first."

The woman appears to be young, and she's usually seen in the nursery, which is the room one surgeon chose to perform surgery. This room bears the most graphic bloodstains in the house; in front of the window are the bloody outlines of shoeprints. It's where the surgeon stood as he executed his grisly craft for 48 straight hours.

Mrs. Seiberling told Shelly and Maddie that no one knows who she is but they suspect she may have been the wife or sweetheart of a soldier who died at Carnton. She is usually heard quietly crying, hence the name.

I asked Shelly, "Was she crying? Did you hear her weeping?"

"Margie," Shelly said, "She was facing out the window. We couldn't see her face and we sure weren't going to wait around to find out!"

It has been many years since Shelly's ghostly summer at Carnton, and yet, she says, "It still gives me chills."

Little Angels

John and Carrie McGavock had five children of whom three died before the age of 13. Before the 20th century and the development of penicillin, childhood mortality rates stood about 50 percent. Carrie and John lost John Randal in 1854 at three months of age, Mary Elizabeth in 1858 at six years, and Martha in 1862 at 12. Hattie and Winder, born in 1855 and 1857 respectively, did survive well past middle age.

The two older children died at home, but Mary Elizabeth was visiting with her family in Louisiana when she passed away. A doctor's letter dated January 18, 1858, informed that she had a "disease of the heart, which doubtless will bring her to an early grave." She died eight days later. A marker in the family cemetery bears her name, but it's not certain that she is actually buried there because of the logistics of transporting a body in those days. Some observers have wondered if she's still trying to get home.

The photograph, right, that also appears on the cover of this book was taken by a guest on a Carnton ghost tour in 2005. It wasn't until later when she viewed this photo on the computer that she noticed a figure in a ground floor window. Even skeptics admit there's something there; believers see a little girl facing to the side wearing a bonnet and holding a doll.

I led the tour that night and I can promise you that when she took the photo there was no one in the house and there had not been any such child on the tour that night.
-- MGT

*Photograph courtesy of
Amy Price, © 2005.*

Reenactors camping on the grounds after participating in a living history presentation at Carnton in the early 2000s were awakened by laughter in the middle of the night. They thought the sound was coming from the cemetery but then realized it was from the house. One man looked in a window and saw a young girl holding the hand of a smaller boy. He said they were laughing and smiling together. One of the men took a picture of the house but didn't notice anything odd until he got his pictures developed and saw what looks like a young girl looking out the same window. Both agreed she looked about six years old.

A family reenacted living history at Carnton five years ago. One member of the family, a girl of six, stopped an employee and told her, "I just saw a little girl floating down the stairs."

"Oh, really?" the employee asked. "What did she look like?"

"She had short dark hair and was six, like me," the girl answered.

A circa 1856 daguerreotype taken two years before Mary Elizabeth died depicts Martha and Mary Elizabeth, 4 at the time, with short dark hair.

A tour guide recently saw a similar child at Carnton.

"We were just finishing up in the dining room and I asked if anyone had questions," the guide said.

A little girl piped up, "My name is Sarah. I'm six years old."

"Hi Sarah," the guide said.

The guide was about to lead her group into the center hall when she saw a very different little girl running there.

"I saw a little girl wearing black stockings and boots, and a light-colored pinafore-type dress. She had short dark hair and appeared to be about six years old," the guide recalled. "She ran from the plantation office toward the best parlor. She took two steps before fading away. But it wasn't as if someone were turning down the dimmer switch. She disappeared in the blink of an eye."

Carnton's center hall is hung with wallpaper reproduced from the paper that hung there during the Civil War years. A little girl skipped across the hall one day not long ago and disappeared into thin air.

The door from the plantation office into the hall is kept locked or chained. Later the guide asked the other tour guide in the house if he had any children on his tour. He had not.

The guide treasures this experience. "Mary Elizabeth wasn't running away from us because she was scared. She had a pleasant expression. Playful. I think she was getting out of our way; she knows my routine. I feel that she must have heard the little girl talking and that's why she appeared that day."

Later the guide reflected, "She was running on the center hall floor. You would have heard footsteps if it had been a real person. She made not a sound."

A Haunting Melody

In the mid-1990s the Ely family of Franklin visited Carnton one October evening just as light was waning and encountered a very different specter.

Josh Ely, ten years old at the time, had visited Carnton earlier that day with his fourth grade class at Walnut Grove Elementary School in Franklin. The school together with Carnton provides an interactive and hands-on Civil War experience for the students. The boys sport Civil War uniforms and the girls don pioneer outfits, complete with pinafores and bonnets. They bring lunch in tin pails and pitch canvas tents, just like the soldiers did. They always enjoy their special day.

When Josh got home from school he was so exuberant about his day at Carnton that he convinced his parents, Liz and John, to visit Carnton that evening. They arrived about 5 p.m., just as the director was leaving for the day.

She leaned out her car window as they passed on the dusty gravel road leading to the house off Carnton Lane, and told them that the site was closed and everyone was gone, but that they were welcome to wander around the grounds until it got dark.

The Elys parked their car next to the visitor center and walked up to the wide porch that extends along the back of the house. They listened as Josh told them all about the bloodstains on the floor and the arms and legs being tossed out the window. They left the porch and walked around the west side of the house toward the front, when they began to hear the faint but stirring strings of a violin.

"We could not figure out where the sound was coming from," John said. They looked out toward the wide-open fields spreading at the front of the house and saw nothing that could produce such a sound.

"Finally, we realized it was coming from the house."

So the family walked up onto the front porch. First they looked through the side windows next to the front door and saw no sign of life or music. Then they leaned over to the right side to look in the window of the plantation office and saw nothing there. Finally, they looked into the window on the left side into the best parlor. There, sitting in a rocking chair, was a grizzled old Confederate soldier playing the fiddle.

"It was a sad song, a sort of funeral dirge," John recalls. "It was very old-fashioned."

The family stared, entranced, as the old veteran finished the piece, and then slowly rose from the chair, picked up his Confederate officer's hat, and carried his fiddle and bow out of the room toward the family parlor.

"He didn't walk, he floated," John said. "His skin color and the color of his uniform were the same, sort of monochromatic with no coloration to speak of."

The McGavocks entertained guests in this room, called the best parlor. There was a grand piano and flute, and one October night, a fiddle played by an old Confederate army officer.

It took a second, but the Elys straightened up, rubbed their eyes, and asked each other, "Did you see that? Was that really a soldier we saw there playing the fiddle?"

They all agreed they had seen just that.

Then wondering where he had gone and hoping to see him again, they walked back around to the other porch and looked in as many windows as they could. They saw no one. They walked away from the house to see if they could make anything out in the upstairs windows. Nothing. They finally tried the doors and they were locked tight. As the minutes ticked by it got darker and darker, and was finally pitch black when the Elys left. No lights ever came on in the house. They were finally convinced they had seen a ghost.

As far as the spirit's identity, no one at Carnton knows of any McGavock family member who played the fiddle. Furthermore, no one in the immediate family was a Confederate soldier. Perhaps it was just a soldier who died in the house, and appreciating the family's hospitality, never wanted to leave.

Over the years, reports are legion of phantom Confederate soldiers marching across the fields surrounding Carnton or riding atop galloping horses in a frenzy of activity or loudly pacing the porch.

Similar stories have come from the volunteers who drop by Carnton in the middle of the night during the week before the annual Heritage Ball. They are just checking to make sure no one is making mischief with the tent and decorations that are on the site in preparation for the event. Sometimes these volunteers have the fright of their lives.

Other times the visits are surreptitious. One day when I was at work at Carnton a young neighbor of mine named Laura Baxter brought her friend Allie to see me and told me an interesting story along just those lines.

"I have a paper to write and I want to write it about the ghosts of Carnton," Allie told me.

"Ok," I said, "Is this a subject you're interested in?"

"Well," she said, "Actually I am."

"I take it you've had personal experience," I told her. "Out with it!"

Allie Pierce and a friend named Brittany decided to pay a nighttime visit to Carnton when they were in high school. They arrived at Carnton about midnight and because the site was closed, drove up the drive to the house with their headlights off, excited to be doing a little amateur ghost-hunting. When they got to the house they turned on the headlights and shined them toward the house.

"We didn't see anything," Allie said. "We said, 'This is stupid.'"

So they decided to leave. Brittany tried to restart the car but it wouldn't crank. The engine was dead.

"Then some interior lights started flashing in the car," Allie said. "I don't know what it could have been; it seemed like some lights around the dashboard."

Then they saw the ghosts.

"There were two people on the porch. They looked like soldiers, wearing officer hats."

Brittany frantically tried to start the car and it finally turned over. "We high-tailed it out of there," Allie said.

They made some phone calls and recruited two friends to make a return visit.

Within the hour they were back at Carnton. Creeping slowly up the gravel drive toward the house, "all of a sudden we drove into a fogbank. It was really bizarre, and seemed to come from nowhere," Allie said. "Everyone else was looking at the house where the most fog was but I was looking toward the fields when I saw him."

"Him" was a Union soldier sitting on a hay bale.

"I told everybody to look and everybody turned and saw him. Brittany screamed bloody murder and started to drive out across the field toward him. As we got closer he disappeared in the headlights.

"Then we saw more soldiers, a couple dozen of them. They were both Union and Confederate. We were within feet of them. Some were wearing hats, some were not.

"They were standing in formation, not moving. We could not see faces but we could make out hair. We were so close we could see the color of their uniforms.

"The whole episode took less than a minute. We could not get out of there fast enough." Allie said. "We were screaming and crying and shaking all the way home."

Terrified at first, Allie now considers her Carnton experiences exciting. "There is nothing malicious or malevolent about the ghosts at Carnton. I think they're actually more like echoes, replaying the past. Memories. It's always going on but sometimes you see it and sometimes you don't. You have to be in the right place at the right time and be somewhat perceptive. Not gullible, just open-minded."

One former tour guide was not open-minded until the day he was in the guest bedroom about to open the jib window to go out onto the second story porch. A jib window has a double hung window on top and a short door on the bottom. The window is raised, and the door opened, and then the window is transformed into a door.

He was facing the window, about to raise it, when he felt a presence behind him and heard a voice softly say twice, "Let me help you with that; let me help you with that."

The window flew up.

Denny Blake, another former tour guide, was in the room showing her group the jib window when she looked onto the porch.

"The eight rocking chairs are out there, and about every other rocking chair was rocking," Denny said. "The ones that were rocking moved just like the way my grandmother used to

Carnton's back porch was added in the 1840s. It's the perfect place to rock, whether anyone's there or not.

rock in her rocking chair. The other chairs were still. All the ladies on the tour looked and shrieked when they saw it happen."

Respect Thy Ghosts

A Carnton employee who was somewhat close-minded on the subject of ghosts and vocal about it, was one day asked to return those rocking chairs to the upstairs porch after a winter in the attic. He brought eight chairs down from the attic and placed them all in the guest room, preparing to take them one at a time out the jib window.

He finished his task, and turned to leave the room. When he came to the door, it was shut and the heavy oak guest chamber pot was in front of the door inside the room.

The facts are as follows: The door opens into the room. The chamber pot is inside the room. There's not another door into the room except from the porch, and the employee was in and out of that door the whole time he was in the room. I know what you're thinking: that's not possible. But that's the way it happened.

"I didn't really think anything of this, moved the chamber pot and went out the door. As I was going downstairs, I thought maybe someone had tried to play a prank on me," he said.

"I then realized that I was the only one upstairs at the time and that the door opened to the inside of the bedroom. It was physically impossible to place the chamber pot firmly in front of the door. It suddenly occurred to me I had experienced something that so many others claimed to have experienced: an encounter with one of the spirits at Carnton Plantation.

"I guess lucky for me, this one was in a playful mood."

A former tour guide did not find her experience "playful" at all. Here in her own words:

> *Working as a tour guide at historic Carnton Plantation was one of the highlights of my life. I love history and was excited about sharing the stories of the family's history and the soldiers that spent time there when the house was a field hospital during the Civil War.*
>
> *Unfortunately, some tourists weren't interested in the facts; they wanted to hear the ghost stories.*
>
> *After a year and a half as a guide, I didn't have any ghost stories. I just hadn't had an "experience." One day, a fellow tour guide was leading guests on the final tour of the day. I seized the opportunity to give the tourists what they'd truly come for. I crept into the parlor to peck out a short melody on the old square grand piano. Having known they were the only ones in the house at the time, I peeked through the crack of the door to see their faces . . . mouths wide open, staring at one another in disbelief.*
>
> *"Did you hear that?" the tourists asked the guide. The guide seemed as astonished as the tourists, as this was apparently his first "experience," too.*

I simply could not resist. I went back to the piano and played a few more notes. The guide and the guests came running to the parlor as I slipped behind the door. By this time, my hand was cupped over my nose and mouth. I couldn't bear it. I was in stitches. They left . . . having gotten exactly what most guests crave on their tour . . . a ghostly experience at Carnton.

It was nearing closing time so I decided to go ahead and lock up the house, which was my typical late-afternoon routine. I came back downstairs, set the security alarm and went to the door. I turned the old skeleton key to unlock the door and leaned forward to pull the door open. Suddenly I heard the old wood floor creak behind me, as if someone were walking across it. I froze in my tracks, reassured that I was the only person remaining in the house.

Then it happened. Hovering over me was the presence of something I will never forget. As if it had simply walked up behind me, stood against my back and was waiting for me to let us both out. Every hair on my arms stood up and it felt like the weight of another human being was pressing against me. I couldn't get the door opened fast enough! My little prank had backfired. Now I was the one getting the ghostly Carnton experience! After nearly two years of waiting for proof of ghostly existence at Carnton, the joke was on me.

--Former Tour Guide, 2006

Turnabout is Fair Play

Carnton, as well as all of the other houses and buildings discussed in this book, is private property. Signs around Carnton make clear that trespassing after hours is not permitted. The police patrol the grounds and violators can be arrested. The alarm system on the house and visitor center is wired to the police station, and the police are quick to respond. A former executive director asked me to include the following story in all my ghost tours when I gave them at Carnton, and I also want to include it here as a caution to would-be late night ghost hunters.

The mother of a Carnton bride came to see me three week before her daughter's wedding, panicked and worried.

"I just heard a story from my son Seth and if Ashley hears it she will insist that we move the wedding," Brenda said.

What in the world? I couldn't imagine what was coming.

"Seth and a friend who lives in Polk Place [the neighborhood south of Carnton], sneaked over ghost-hunting one night when Seth was spending the night at his house," she said.

"They were on the front porch, and the friend looked in the window and saw a ghost. He screamed, and he ran all the way back to Polk Place, jumped the fence, ran upstairs, jumped in bed and pulled the covers over his eyes."

Yikes!

"Yes, and he was so scared he says it took him about 30 minutes to get his nerve up to come out from under the covers. When he did, the ghost was standing there at the end of his bed. He thinks he fainted."

I assured Brenda that we'd never had a ghost interrupt a wedding and that I was sure Ashley would never hear about it from us. In the end the wedding went off without a hitch . . . actually, *with* a hitch.

With Carnton's gruesome history some might wonder why couples want to have the most important day of their lives commemorated there. I believe I know why and it's not just because of its physical beauty, although that's certainly a huge factor. Carnton has an authenticity that cannot be manufactured. Its history gives it substance and depth. I believe that's why so many brides and grooms choose Carnton, exchanging their vows under the magnificent Osage orange tree in the restored historic garden or on one of the porches. They are seeking a place that has meaning on the most meaningful day of their lives. I heard that dozens of times.

Carnton was witness to struggle, suffering and death. If any house on earth should be haunted, it would be Carnton. Yet most visitors (except the unauthorized nocturnal type) leave

Carnton feeling calm, peaceful and contented. Carrie watches still . . . .

Carnton's garden was restored in the 1990s to its appearance during Carrie McGavock's lifetime.

Chapter 11

The Final Resting Place

T he Battle of Franklin dead were hastily buried the day after the battle in shallow, makeshift graves on the land where they fell. Marked with wooden headboards, these graves deteriorated rapidly, and the land where they lay was needed by its owners for cultivation.

In response, in the spring of 1866, Carrie and John McGavock donated two acres adjoining their family cemetery to reinter the Confederate soldiers killed in the Battle of Franklin. The bodies of the Union dead had already been moved to the national cemetery in Murfreesboro.

The donation is impressive, even more so when one considers that after the war, the needs of the living trumped any obligation to the dead. All over the country, soldiers endeavored to eke out a living minus a leg or two and/or an arm or two. Southern states devoted a large percentage of their budgets to provide prosthetic limbs for their veterans. Who could afford to establish a cemetery?

Snow shrouds the graves of 1,481 Confederate soldiers killed at the Battle of Franklin at the McGavock Confederate Cemetery.

The McGavocks had lost some of their wealth and the future was uncertain, but they stepped up. Forming a committee and soliciting donations, they hired George, Polk and Marcellus Cuppett, three brothers who had served in the Confederate army as Texas Rangers, and who happened to be in Franklin at the time, to oversee the exhumation and identification of the bodies.

Amazingly, the Cuppetts identified two thirds of the soldiers, about 1,000 of the 1,481 bodies reinterred in the McGavock Confederate cemetery.

Carrie McGavock kept a cemetery journal detailing information about the dead and carried it with her on daily visits to the cemetery, meeting with soldiers' families and later, veterans who returned to the place where so many of their brethren lost their lives. Veterans' reunions were held regularly and were always well-attended, by veterans from both North and South.

When the McGavocks were alive the cemetery was well-maintained, but after their deaths (John in 1893 and Carrie in 1905) its condition declined. During the 20th century vandalism and theft contributed to its plight. Today the cemetery is meticulously maintained by the United Daughters of the Confederacy, Franklin Chapter 14, to welcome the tens of thousands of people who visit every year.

Many of the visitors come at night, as cemeteries are popular sites for ghost-hunting. Again, be aware that the cemetery is open only during daylight hours.

Remember Allie and her friends?

One night they paid a visit to the cemetery but didn't go inside. They stayed on the circular drive in front of it. All of a sudden, Allie smelled fire.

"At first I thought it was my car on fire, and we jumped out of the car. Then I realized it wasn't that kind of a fire. It was more like a campfire smell. It was really strong. Then I got the feeling that someone was watching and didn't want us there. So we left."

Carter Page made a nocturnal visit to the cemetery on the anniversary of the Battle of Franklin several years ago and had quite a fright. Like Allie, he didn't go into the cemetery. He walked out into the field next to the cemetery.

"No more than five minutes out there in the field I heard the sound of what seemed to be battle cries," Carter said. "I could tell it was screaming of soldiers but it was muffled . . . a whisper to my ears but I could definitely tell it was the screams of battle."

He quickly returned to his car, then decided to go back out in the field.

This time, "The pressure was a hundred times worse than before. My head was absolutely pounding and I was very uneasy—then it happened. I had gone no more than 30 yards from the car when I physically could not take another step. I was stone cold and something felt like it was keeping me from moving any closer down the cemetery. It felt as if someone were standing right in front of me and was not allowing me to go forward. I started to panic and without actually hearing any audible sound I heard a voice telling me to go away and not to take another step."

He returned to his car and left.

Other guests have reported seeing soldiers marching throughout the cemetery. One reenactor doing maintenance work there recalled seeing another reenactor—at least that's what he thought—in the cemetery. When he called out to him, the man walked off in the other direction and disappeared behind a tree.

Angie Johnson was new to Franklin in 2004 when she signed up to play a night golf tournament at the Country Club of Franklin. The 110-acre golf course, which closed the following year, abutted Carnton and the Confederate cemetery and is part of the battlefield of Franklin. In fact, if you visit today (in 2012), you'll still see the remnants of the club: tennis courts, a clubhouse and the landforms that indicate fairways, tees and greens.

About midnight, Angie had run out of the glow-in-the-dark balls used in night tournaments, so she left the course and went to her truck to get more. As she approached her truck, which was parked against the fence around the cemetery, she noticed a group of people standing inside around a grave.

"There were between 10-12 people: men, women and one little boy," Angie recollects. "They were very solemn, very quiet, dressed in Civil War-era clothing. Some men were wearing uniforms, others civilian clothes. One man had on a black suit, white shirt, and thin black tie. Some were wearing hats. I couldn't understand what anyone was saying, but I thought it was a funeral. It seemed like a preacher conducting a funeral service."

Angie's next thought was that it had to be some kind of reenactment. She watched for a minute, mesmerized by what she saw. The reenactors gave no indication that they saw *her* though. Angie then grabbed some golf balls, and ran back to her foursome, including the club's pro. She told them that she'd just seen a reenactment in the cemetery.

"No way," they told her. "There are no reenactments in the cemetery at this time of night. You've got to be kidding."

Angie insisted, and quickly dragged the other golfers back to the cemetery. No one was there. Everyone had disappeared. And then she realized it didn't make sense. A reenactment at midnight? And who brings a six-year-old boy to a cemetery in the middle of the night? And what Angie didn't know at the time is that nobody has been buried at this cemetery in nearly 100 years.

Angie was shocked. She had just seen what had appeared to be flesh-and-blood people a few minutes before and now they had now disappeared. She took some razzing from her foursome, but she's convinced today that she saw not reenactors, but ghosts.

Scents of a Spirit

I promised a personal story and here it is. It took place in the cemetery. I was finishing up a ghost tour at Carnton and had taken my group into the family cemetery. As I walked up to the grave of Sarah and Randal McGavock, the builder of Carnton, I smelled flowers. My first thought was lilacs. I mentioned this to the guest who was closest to me, saying, "The lilacs smell lovely right now." She looked at me as if to say, "I don't think so." It was late November. There are no lilacs, or anything else for that matter, blooming in November. That's all it was, but I will say the scent didn't make sense.

People who study paranormal activities say that olfactory phenomena are more common than visual and auditory ones. Over the years at Carnton numerous guests touring the house have claimed to smell blood, ammonia, flowers and even roast pork. Some guests are so overcome they have to leave the tour. Two policemen told me they smelled a very strong scent of flowers at a defined spot on the brick walkway between the visitor center and the back porch of the house. The garden is less than 15 yards away, but as they walked toward it, the smell became fainter and fainter. They described the smell as like being in a flower shop.

Denny Blake was on a ghost tour one night when she and the guide leading the tour smelled something—but couldn't figure out what. The tour was in Carnton's guest bedroom at the time, and Denny was standing next to a closet where guests usually don't stand.

"The first smell was a sickly sweet odor," Denny said. "Then it was as if gunpowder exploded under my nose."

A guest on tour suggested sulfur. Ah ha! The guide had lit candles. Matches explained the sulfur smell. But no, she had used a butane lighter.

Later Denny described the experience to her sister. She suggested Denny had disturbed the spirit of a man lighting his pipe stuffed with an old-fashioned cherry tobacco. That would explain both smells.

Carter Page and his uncle visited the cemetery one night while his mother was on a ghost tour of the house.

"We were walking through the graves and I smelled gunpowder. I didn't say anything to my uncle, but then he asked, 'Do you smell that? It smells like gunpowder.'

"We could actually follow the smell, and there was absolutely no one else around."

AFTERWORD

I hope you've enjoyed these ghost stories I've collected over the past nine years. My favorite story, however, doesn't involve anything supernatural or paranormal. It really doesn't belong in a ghost book. Nevertheless, I want to share it here.

Shortly after I began working at Carnton in 2004 a retired couple visited the site. They took a tour of the house and then came in the gift shop.

"We're from New York State," the woman said, "and we're looking for the grave of my great-great-great-great-uncle who fought and died at the Battle of Franklin.

"Your ancestor would be buried in Murfreesboro at the national cemetery," I explained. "The Union soldiers are buried there. It's only the Confederates who are here."

"You don't understand," she said. "I have a Confederate ancestor."

I didn't expect that. Here's her story.

In the late 1960s, the woman's parents decided to sell the farm in upstate New York that had been in their family for many generations. The parents told their children that they would have one more opportunity to explore the old homeplace. So the children, who were young adults at the time, paid a last visit.

First they wandered through the house, enjoying the memories of their childhoods, and chose a few things to keep as keepsakes. Then they went out to the barn.

"We were poking around, just looking around the barn, when for the first time we noticed a false wall at the back of the barn," the woman said. "This was a total surprise. We had never noticed this before. So of course we wanted to investigate."

"We pulled the boards away and discovered a trunk. That was a further surprise. All these years and nobody ever discovered it. We brought the trunk inside and opened it; we had to break the lock to get in. We began to go through it. It was full of old stuff. We couldn't believe what it was."

"It was the clothing, papers and personal belongings of a relative, who turned out to be a fourth great uncle. And as we looked at the papers we discovered something utterly shocking. He was a Confederate soldier. We had a Confederate ancestor."

"This was just unbelievable to us. As New Yorkers, we weren't expecting that. Upstate New York was such staunch Union territory. We just could not imagine how anyone from here could change allegiance and fight against the United States.

But as we read through the papers, we discovered what happened."

This great-great-great-great-uncle, they learned, had in the 1850s as a young man headed south to seek his fortune in Charleston, South Carolina, then the wealthiest city in the country. After he lived there for a time, he became a South Carolinian. By the time the war broke out, and Fort Sumter was fired upon, he had become a true Southerner. He joined the Confederate army.

He fought with the Confederacy for three years and eight months, finally catching a bullet in Franklin, Tennessee. He died on the battlefield of Franklin.

Someone notified his family that he died in the terrible battle at Franklin. His mother wept. To everybody else, the rest of his family, his neighbors and friends in his home state of New York, he was a traitor. He had committed treason against his country.

So his mother had to mourn in private. Then she took all of his clothing, papers and personal belongings and placed them in a trunk, along with a quilt she made from his silk ties and handkerchiefs. She had a false wall built in the barn on the family's farm and placed the trunk filled with her son's belongings behind it. It rested undiscovered nearly 100 years.

The woman continued:

"We finally understood. He had moved south and become part of the South. That's why he fought on the side of the South. And most of all we realized how hard it was for his mother, who loved him but could not mourn him publicly. She had to hide her tears and sorrow."

"We always wanted to go to the place he had died, but it's so far out here from New York. We didn't know if we'd find anything here, if anything was left of the battlefield. Finally, we're retired, and now we're here. We see the cemetery. Can you help us find his grave?"

I asked his name. They gave it to me. We looked it up in Carrie's book and found his grave in the South Carolina section. They walked out to the cemetery and found the small white limestone marker engraved with his initials. They mourned at the grave of an ancestor they never knew for the mother who never could. Their journey was complete. Carrie McGavock's legacy lives on after 145 years.

Carrie McGavock's cemetery marker at Carnton.

The Tennessee dead lie closest to the McGavocks
family graves at Carnton.

I started the book with a poem, and I'll end with another one:

Flanders Fields

In Flanders fields the poppies blow
Between the crosses, row on row
That mark our place; and in the sky
The larks, still bravely singing, fly
Scarce heard amid the guns below.

We are the Dead. Short days ago
We lived, felt dawn, saw sunset glow,
Loved and were loved, and now we lie
    In Flanders fields.

Take up our quarrel with the foe:
To you from failing hands we throw
The torch; be yours to hold it high.
If ye break faith with us who die
We shall not sleep, though poppies grow
    In Flanders fields.

--John McCrae, 1915

ABOUT THE AUTHOR

Margie Gould Thessin is the owner and co-founder of Franklin on Foot, offering guided walking tours in historic Franklin, Tennessee since 2003.

Margie graduated from the University of Florida (B.A.; history) and Catholic University (J.D.) After practicing law in West Virginia for seven years, she retired to a life of child-rearing and volunteerism in Franklin, which led her to the Heritage Classroom program where she served as teacher from 1998-2004. She was director of sales and marketing at Carnton Plantation from 2004-2007 and served as Interim Executive Director from June, 2008-August, 2009. Margie is a member of the Franklin Battlefield Preservation Commission. She is the author of *Lizzie's War*, a historical novel for children based on the experiences of real Franklin children during the Civil War.

Seen here among the graves at one of her favorite haunts, Franklin's old City Cemetery, Margie Thessin never met a cemetery she didn't like.

ABOUT FRANKLIN ON FOOT

Franklin on Foot offers a variety of tours for just about every age and interest—even if you think you hate history. We call it "edu-tainment," our special blend of education and entertainment that appeals to almost everyone. We don't recite facts or memorize scripts. We tell stories—and who doesn't love a good juicy story!

FOF's tours include ghost, crime, historic, cemetery and Civil War themes, as well as children's programs and activities, both in school and out. We have bike tours and rentals and food tours. We can do driving tours for the mobility-challenged, as well as to visit areas outside walking and biking distance.

We could tell you we do great tours—but we'll let our visitors tell you instead.

Scenic Franklin Bike Tour: My husband and I took the Bike Tour of Franklin with Margie! It was a beautiful ride through Franklin with Margie stopping and telling us information about the town, the history and the people throughout the ride! It was one of the best tours we have ever taken! I would recommend this to everyone!!! Margie is a wonderful storyteller and she makes the history of the town come alive! Tripadvisor.com review

Haunted Franklin Tour: We had gone on the tour last year. It was so enjoyable we called this year to see if the tour would be different. They said they had hundreds of different stories; so they would change the route. It was very different. They mix a lot of history, in with the ghost stories; so if you have somebody along that doesn't care for the ghost stories; they will enjoy the history. Make sure you go early enough in your visit, to go back to the buildings the next day. You will want to; after hearing the history. I am planning a trip back, to do the history tour, and the food tour. Tripadvisor.com review

Southern Style Food Tour: My wife and I had relatives in town from Birmingham. They love Civil War history and we thought this would be a good way to let them learn some history and eat some great food. We were not disappointed. The 3-hour tour took us to six great restaurants in Historic Franklin. We sampled some great food. No one will need dinner tonight. Great idea for out of town visitors. Margie knows her history and is a GREAT tour guide. Tripadvisor.com review

Classic Franklin Tour: My wife and I were celebrating our 5 yr and I was trying to think of something fun to do. I found this and after reading the reviews, I signed us up. My wife had no idea till we got to Franklin what exactly we were doing. I was nervous she would not have a good time, but it ended up being great. Our guide was wonderful and the city of Franklin is a cool town. Sign up, you won't regret it. Tripadvisor.com review

Haunted Franklin Tour: My girlfriends and I wanted to do something different on a Saturday night. We took the Franklin on Foot Ghost Tour. Anna was wonderful! She knows so much about the area and grew up in Franklin. This tour is full of historical facts that make the information come to life. I wish all history was this interesting with the personal stories. I plan on taking all my future visitors (family and friends) on this tour when they come to visit us. I am ready to take more tours of Franklin on Foot. Tripadvisor.com review

Haunted Franklin Tour: Thank you so very much for an excellent evening! My husband and I have taken similarly themed tours in New Orleans, Chicago, Savannah, and Charleston. The Haunted Franklin tour ranks as one of the best we have taken. Our guide was very knowledgeable, witty, and entertaining. The material seemed to us to be extremely well researched.

Classic Franklin, Haunted Franklin and Murder and Mayhem tours: Having recently relocated to Franklin and desiring to learn a bit about the area, we have taken three fun-filled and incredibly affordable tours with Franklin on Foot. Outstanding narration of the history of the town, little-known facts of the buildings, events and personalities that have made Franklin what it is, great ghost stories and "ghouly" happenings add to the fun!

Civil War Tour: Your tour guide was able to put the battle into the broader context and we all finally understood the significance of the battle and how it all fit together.

School Programs: As an educator, I am always searching for hands-on, stimulating activities for students. Margie Thessin and Rene Evans have visited my classes several times and have always brought history to life! Their ability to share their wealth of knowledge in age-appropriate and interesting lessons always result in students learning and wanting them to visit again. These two ladies and their talents are true Franklin treasures!

Haunted Franklin tour: The tour was unlike anything I have ever experienced. I learned so much about Franklin's history, while simultaneously being entertained by the hair-raising tales told by our wonderfully animated tour guide.

Classic Franklin tour: The best walking tour, bar none, that I have ever been on.

Haunted Franklin tour: I have taken ghost tours in Charleston, Savannah and Franklin this summer, and the Franklin tour was the best by far! Great job, Franklin on Foot!

Classic Franklin tour: As a former curator and docent at a historic house museum in Raleigh, N.C., I enjoy taking tours elsewhere. I am so impressed with the professional and interesting tour the guide gave. She had so much information and did such a great job telling the stories.

Haunted Franklin and Murder and Mayhem tours: We took the Haunted Franklin tour at 7 p.m. and the Murder and Mayhem tour at 9 p.m., all on the same day. We loved it! We would highly recommend either of these tours to anyone with an interest in history, ghosts and wonderful storytelling!

For more information, view www.franklinonfoot.com
or call 615-400-3808. Check out all our reviews on Tripadvisor.com

FRANKLIN'S UNKNOWN SOLDIER

The last funeral for a Civil War soldier in Franklin took place October 10, 2009. The remains, which included Civil War uniform buttons and a bullet, were found at a construction site in May, 2009. After a funeral at St. Paul's Episcopal Church, the remains were reinterred with full military honors in front of over several thousand people at Franklin's Rest Haven cemetery, his identity known only to God . . .

CPSIA information can be obtained
at www.ICGtesting.com
Printed in the USA
LVHW111439010219
606090LV00001B/210/P

9 781434 899828